WHO WOULD BUY THIS? The Archie McPhee Story
Mark L. Pahlow
With Gibson Holub & David Wahl

The Accoutrements Publishing Co.
PO Box 30811
Seattle, WA 98113

Book Design: Gibson Holub, David Wahl & Scott King
Photography: Scott King

ISBN-10: 0-9786649-7-3
ISBN-13: 978-0-9786649-7-8
Library of Congress Control Number: 2008907304

Printed in China

www.mcphee.com

# WHO
# WOULD

The Archie McPhee Story

# BUY
# THIS?

**MARK PAHLOW**

With Gibson Holub & David Wahl

# CONTENTS

# INTRODUCTION

Archie McPhee was created because reality just wasn't living up to my expectations. Let me explain.

Having been born and raised in Ohio, I understand boredom in a profound way. In 1963, the two most exciting things in my life were my $3.98 "Made In Japan" transistor radio with a fake leather case and Whitey, my albino hamster. I did my best to liven things up. For instance, my brother Herb and I hooked an aluminum lawn chair up to a train transformer one summer's evening and charged the other kids in the neighborhood a nickel to get electrocuted. I made a nice profit and, thankfully, no one died.

For summer vacations, my family would drive our 1957 Ford Fairlane to Sedalia, Missouri to visit relatives. Fireworks were legal in Missouri, so I'd buy as many as I could and smuggle them back to Ohio where they were illegal. A single "lady finger" firecracker that cost me 1/100th of a cent could quickly be resold for ten cents — a markup of 10,000%. I made a mint until the local police put a stop to my thriving business, which turned out to be a forewarning of my clashes to come with "The Man" while trying to engage in honest commerce.

Growing up I entertained myself with a steady diet of Mad Magazine, late night horror movies hosted by Cleveland celebrity, Ghoulardi, and comic books. Even at a young age, I found myself more attracted to the ads for x-ray specs and Sea-Monkeys® than the latest exploits of Casper the Friendly Ghost.

After high school, I hitchhiked through 25 countries in Europe and Africa in search of meaning, taking work where I could get it. During that time I quit or was fired from a variety of strange jobs like dressing up in a full Viking outfit to sell sweaters from the Faeroe Islands, filling cans of shellac and affixing their lids in a factory and separating egg yolks as they passed on a fast conveyer belt (good ones into the chute for baby food; bad ones into the chute for shampoo). Upon returning to America and working for the U.S. Department of Commerce as a census enumerator, I had to admit I was unemployable in modern society. Yet, I knew there was a place for me somewhere.

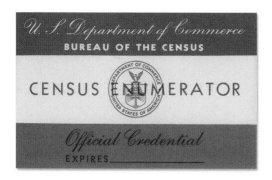

All I needed was a way to make enough money to buy brown rice, alfalfa sprouts and cat food with enough left over to keep my decrepit, 1965 VW Microbus running. I was living in a society of bewildering conformity gilded with deep superficiality and it was rough. Reality was closing in on me and I wanted to scream.

I moved to California and worked as a night clerk at Lose The Blues Bookstore in Los Angeles. While there, I sold Bob Dylan the complete works of Albert Camus and books by I.B. Singer to people whose wrists were marked with numbers from concentration camps. I used the time to ruminate on life and brainstorm business ideas while watching for shoplifters. The more I thought about it, the more I realized that I'd have to set out on my own, so I decided to return to the free market business successes of my youth.

I started by selling collectible stamps, ephemera such as antique cigar box and citrus labels, old toys and odd things I had made, like t-shirts that said, "Shazam!" in Hebrew. I bought thousands of detailed rubber acupuncture figures from Korea, sold them to head shops and used the profits from that to buy a treasure trove of Shirley Temple photographs. Most of my ventures were successes, like the load of anti-siphon gas caps I bought just before the energy crisis started, but a few were outright failures. One of the worst was a truckload of Spanish language comic books that I thought I could turn around and sell in Mexico, not realizing that the Spanish they used was not in the proper Mexican style.

I named it Archie McPhee, after a great uncle from Bismarck, North Dakota. Archie McPhee was famous for taking the first jazz band, "The North Star Merrymakers," to China as its manager in the 1920s. In addition to admiring his

The Real Archie McPhee

spirit of fun, practical jokes and adventure, I loved the crisp cadence of his name.

The next step was starting a catalog. I did the primitive layout for the first few myself. First, I would take bad black and white photos using my Pentax 35mm Spotmatic. Then the photos, developed by the first Costco in the nation, were taken to Bozotronics in the funky Fremont neighborhood to be made into halftones. After that, I'd cut and paste them onto paper using rather toxic rubber cement. Finally, I'd type out the copy on my trusty IBM Selectric typewriter.

When I discovered that I could pick up some extra money driving cars from Los Angeles to New York for driveaway companies I saw an opportunity. Along the way I bought old toys off the shelves of forgotten stores throughout the Midwest. It was on one of these trips that I discovered the amazing windup hot dog eating man. Once I arrived in Manhattan, I'd deliver the car and then sell my treasures at a huge profit to stores like Mythology on the Upper West Side.

It wasn't until I moved to Seattle in 1982 that I figured out how all these disparate things fit together. I would open my own retail store and sell everything I liked, no matter how ridiculous.

**8092. TEETH TONGS.** Top quality, lifesize false teeth choppers (red gums, white teeth) attached to 7" metal tongs. Many uses! We have heard that a present of one of these to your dentist could result in free gold crowns. $2.95 each. Dental Convention Special: 5 for $10.50. Each in clean, hygienically sealed bag.

**8248. MR. POTATO H**
Wonderful! The old fellow him handy travel size edition... a box small enough to fit in your Each contains 17 different use in building your own Pota tion. Sorry, potato not include Set. Spud Special: 4 Sets Class of '64 Reunion Spud S Sets for $11.95.

The strength in those early catalogs was not in the presentation, but in the writing. Since the pictures were often dark and printed in muddy black and white on cheap newsprint, it was difficult to make out details. My descriptions of the products were often honest statements detailing how terrible the product was or rambling humorous screeds that mentioned the product only in passing. This suited my character and seemed to connect to certain eccentric members of the public. You know who you are.

I came to realize shopping existed to help make people less depressed. And I was determined to help them in this noble undertaking. It was transcendence through commerce, a symbiotic relationship where buyer and seller both danced and each came away the better for it.

When I started the business, there was no shortage of weird, unexplainable items and delightful oddities in the world. I collected and accumulated the discards of corporate America like there was no tomorrow, as protesters rioted in the streets, President Nixon reigned and everyone wore bell-bottom jeans. Archie McPhee was not in the junk business, but in the artifact business, in the dream business.

As time wore on in the 80s, it became harder and harder to find the good stuff. Where were the boxes full of Japanese fuzzy, mechanical bartenders pouring drinks? Where were the government surplus items like the original WWII propaganda posters I found in a barn in Kansas ("When you drive alone, you drive with Hitler")?

What could take the place of the lovely, porcelain hands that once served as latex glove molds in England, that David Gray (AKA Ax Man, amazing finder of wonderful things) once shipped to me? The antique wooden shoe lasts? The genuine and official morgue toe ID tags? The buckets of porcelain teeth and glass taxidermy eyes that came in twenty-eight assorted

**8557. WIND-UP WALKING CHATTERING TEETH.** Perfect companion gift to the #8092 Teeth Tongs. Give both to your dentist and it could mean discount bridgework as well. These red gummed, pearly white teeth are plastic, 2" X 1½". Wind them up and they chatter as they walk about on little pink feet. $2.25 each. American Dental Association Special: Display box of one dozen/$15.50.

**8103. THE ANT WATCH.** Our exclusive plastic watch that contains 3 black ants. Don't worry ... they are plastic ants! Fool everyone with this. What time is it? Time for ants! Sorry adults—they only come in a small size. that fits children's wrists. $2.25 each. Special: set of 3 for $5.95.

sizes and colors? The charming wooden bog shoes from Minnesota? The real bowling pins? Alas, once those fascinating products were gone, they were gone forever.

When Communism fell, we turned a profit as we bought and sold East German flags, Soviet submarine clocks, USSR anti-drinking and anti-Uncle Sam propaganda posters, tapestries of Marx and Lenin, Stalin playing cards and my personal favorite, genuine KGB liquor flasks. We also commercialized the detritus of democracy, such as the "Keep Max Paulovich for Justice," emery boards, and original Nixon-Watergate Whiskey Brand labels. Now it's all but a memory, albeit an important memory. As Santayana said, "A country without a memory is a country of madmen."

Most dear to my heart was the hillbilly line, which included crooked wooden golf clubs and "hillbilly bug killers." I loved all our hillbilly items but they were one of the few treasures that never sold through, a real commercial failure but still, a special intellectual success. After all, you're basically just selling the customer a bundle of sticks. I still have a box of the bug killers in my closet.

Oh, how I ache for those old treasures! They looked so good in the store and filled me with satisfaction. They were truly our dharma.

As these treasures sold out and fewer new ones came in to replace them, reality was, once again, becoming disappointing. To fight against this deficiency, I decided it was time to change the focus of the business from selling other people's ideas to creating and selling my own toys and novelties. Now my dreams would make the world, or at least my world, more meaningful and fun.

Enter Robert Benton. Not only an authorized "Bozo The Clown" performer and Lieutenant in the San Fernando Police Department, but also the owner of Star Merchandise Company, my source for vast amounts of Bozo collectibles, "see behind you" mirrored glasses and plastic ants. In the early 1980s, he took me to Asia and taught me how to import and work directly with Chinese suppliers. I took to this with exuberance as it gave me the means to create original products. Robert Benton is my sensei and I owe him a great deal for his help over the years.

With these contacts and my new expertise, I started creating products and having them made in Hong Kong and Taiwan, and later in China, Vietnam, Sri Lanka and India. These wonderful relationships continue to this day and now I often deal with the sons and daughters of those first Chinese makers I met nearly three decades ago.

To imagine a product, sketch it on a piece of paper, send it overseas and then have it arrive three months later tightly packed in cartons on a big ship from China, was truly thrilling. Reality was once again exciting!

On this page, you see examples of my first attempts at packaging. As you can see, they reveal my limited design skills. However, thanks to a talented group of designers and creative people that have worked for me over the years, the products and packages have improved dramatically.

As the world became more practical, I decided to fight that tendency with the impractical, the useless and the just plain strange. It was a futile and absurd strategy, however, it turned out very, very well for the world and for me.

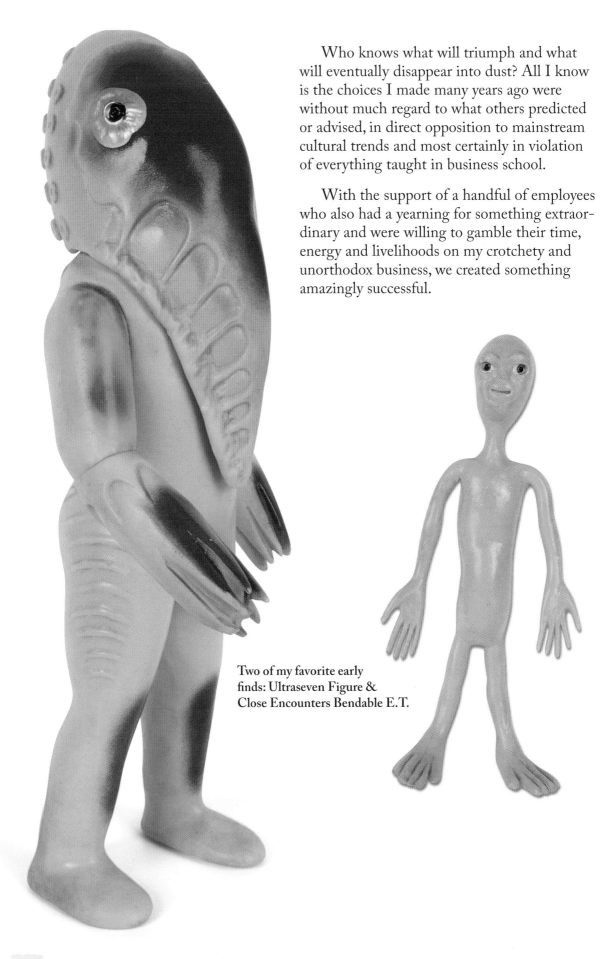

Who knows what will triumph and what will eventually disappear into dust? All I know is the choices I made many years ago were without much regard to what others predicted or advised, in direct opposition to mainstream cultural trends and most certainly in violation of everything taught in business school.

With the support of a handful of employees who also had a yearning for something extraordinary and were willing to gamble their time, energy and livelihoods on my crotchety and unorthodox business, we created something amazingly successful.

Two of my favorite early
finds: Ultraseven Figure &
Close Encounters Bendable E.T.

For some people, the McPhee catalog *is* the product that our company produces. They don't actually buy anything from us; they just want to stay on our mailing list so they can see what kind of crazy thing we'll do next. Of course, we furthered this by putting a dollar value on the cover of each catalog as if it were a magazine. Still, we wonder if there isn't a group of people out there that feel we aren't a real catalog, just a parody of one. Let me be clear about this — we actually sell this stuff.

This book is a record of some of our proudest, and most embarrassing, moments. At one time or another, everything in this book seemed to be a sensible, good idea. In fact, most of them were my favorite thing in the world for at least a day.

The pages labeled, "What Were We Thinking," try to explain what was going on in our heads when we decided to make what turned out to be some of our biggest failures.

The "Busted" pages show how some of our more creative schemes seemed to run afoul of "The Man." Unfortunately, there have been many of these confrontations over the years, which is only to be expected when you put such vitality into your work.

The original catalog write-up is included for most of the items in this book to give you some context as to how we tried to sell this stuff and because most of them are damn funny.

If you have any doubts as to the value of the treasures contained in this book, you need look no further than the archives of the Smithsonian. They decided our catalogs are an important indicator of popular culture in the United States and requested, on official government stationery, we provide them with all the catalogs we ever published so that they could be preserved for future generations.

Never have your tax dollars been better spent.

– Mark Pahlow

**ARCHIE McPHEE EMPORIUM, SEATTLE, WA**

# CLASSICS

These are the all-stars, the best of the best, the products that have stood the test of time and sales. Sometimes we carefully crafted them to be that way, but most of the time the right elements just happened to come together to create something with the perfect blend of strange and memorable.

In some cases, like the Rubber Chicken, the original joke it represents has been lost over time. Others, like the Happy Face Bendy, seem to adopt new meanings with each passing year. One decade's symbol of honest, easy-going happiness is the next decade's ironic comment on the emptiness of a surface-only smile.

These are the masterpieces of the Archie McPhee world and you don't have to go to any stuffy museum or opera house to enjoy them. Bring on the funny!

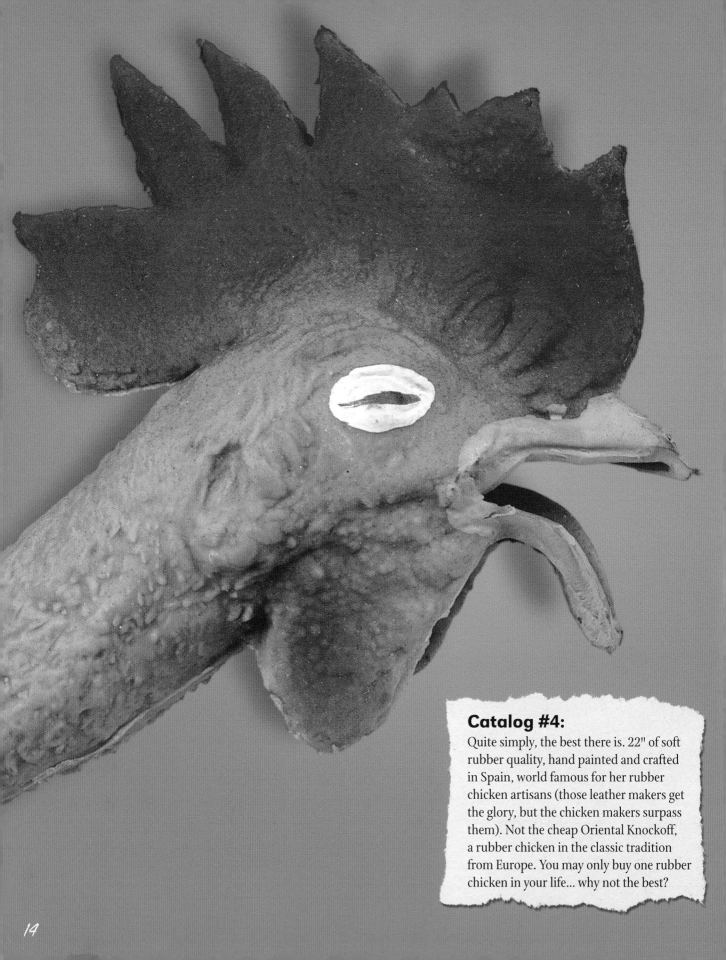

**Catalog #4:**
Quite simply, the best there is. 22" of soft rubber quality, hand painted and crafted in Spain, world famous for her rubber chicken artisans (those leather makers get the glory, but the chicken makers surpass them). Not the cheap Oriental Knockoff, a rubber chicken in the classic tradition from Europe. You may only buy one rubber chicken in your life... why not the best?

# RUBBER CHICKEN

A leftover from a different era, the rubber chicken has become the symbol for humor in America. No one can say for sure why it's funny, but we can say that a high quality rubber chicken is funnier than a low quality one. Our exhaustive search for the best chicken in the world led us to Spain. The Spanish rubber chicken was the finest ever produced, created by craftsman and hand painted by artisans. Gradually the quality drifted downward and the price increased until we finally decided to make our own. We're quite proud of the quality of our new rubber chicken, but we still have a soft spot for the Spanish chicken from the glory days.

Original
Rubber Chicken, 1987

Our Exclusive
Rubber Chicken, 2006

# HAPPY FACE BENDY

Original Design
Sketch, 1988

**BENDY'S TUSHI**

### Catalog #14:

This is the most perfect product we have ever created. Over one year from idea to reality... months of designs, proofs, remakes, critiques, tears and sweat. Now it's here... 6" tall, bright yellow body, white hands and socks, black shoes, belly button and features. Bend him to your will... he submits. Get 2 or 3 and get crazy. We even gave this fellow a tushi. It was the least we could do, considering we don't know whether it's male or female. Arms and legs bend any which way. Perfect for all... young and old, hip and straight, happy and unhappy. Made with the finest materials, the most careful hand production and painting.

Debuted 1989

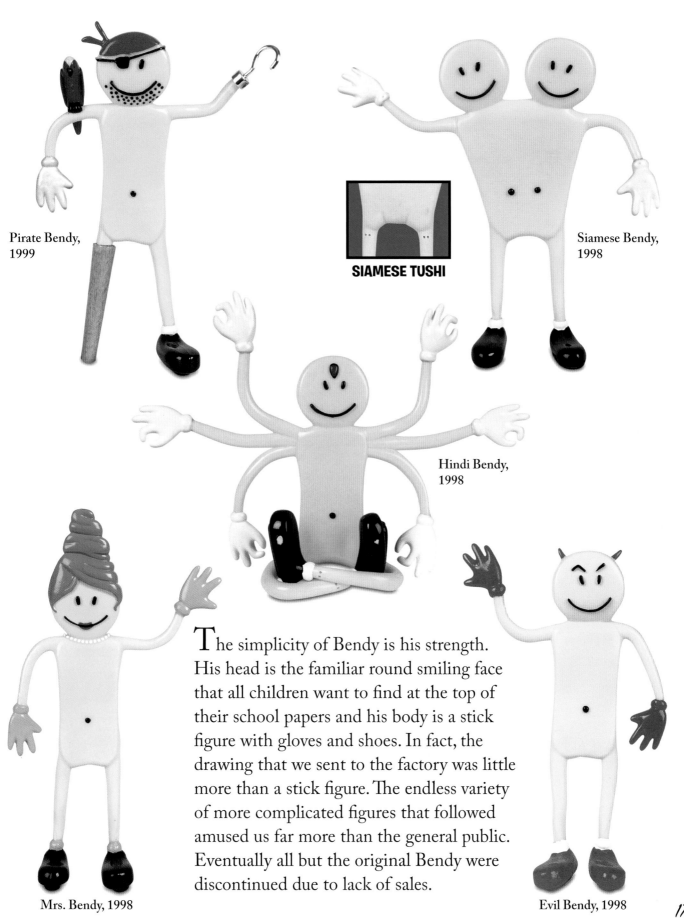

Pirate Bendy,
1999

**SIAMESE TUSHI**

Siamese Bendy,
1998

Hindi Bendy,
1998

The simplicity of Bendy is his strength. His head is the familiar round smiling face that all children want to find at the top of their school papers and his body is a stick figure with gloves and shoes. In fact, the drawing that we sent to the factory was little more than a stick figure. The endless variety of more complicated figures that followed amused us far more than the general public. Eventually all but the original Bendy were discontinued due to lack of sales.

Mrs. Bendy, 1998

Evil Bendy, 1998

Sculpted by Don Featherstone in 1957, plastic Pink Lawn Flamingos became a symbol for tackiness and bad taste — a perfect fit for Archie McPhee! The originals, with Don Featherstone's signature on the rump, are no longer manufactured, making America's yards a little less classy.

# LAWN FLAMINGOS

### Catalog #1:

Go ahead, ruin the neighborhood. Stick them in the yard, on your porch, in a window and don't forget around the tub. One pair (one head up, one head down) per box. Genuine pink plastic. 34" overall height on 21" steel legs. NOTE THE HAND PAINTED HEAD.

Debuted 1985

# POTATO GUN

**Debuted 1985**

### Catalog #1:

Fantastic! Ingenious! Amazing! Place the tip of the barrel into a potato (or zucchini). Withdraw and fire! Shoots harmless spud pellets. Safe to use. Classic design, in full color box with complete instructions for use and care. This is the deluxe, boxed edition. Sorry, potato not included.

One of our all-time best sellers, the Potato Gun is a relic of a time when realistic toy guns were an extremely popular gift to give young boys. The original metal version from Germany could be easily mistaken for an actual gun, but our brightly colored plastic version is obviously a toy. Be careful however, our customers have warned us that the tiny bits of potato it shoots can be difficult to find and, if left to rot, produce a terrible, noxious odor.

# MONSTER WOMEN

## Catalog #33:

These six creatures — half-woman, half-monsters — have come to earth from a distant planet looking for revenge! They saw those old Sinbad movies and thought the hideous monster women looked a little too familiar if you get our drift. These fuming 3" (actual size for their species), rubber figures come in assorted bizarre styles, including Scorpia, Snake Woman and Spider Lady.

Debuted 1994

21

# STYLISH MUSTACHES

Debuted 1999

Bendable Party Mustache, 2005

Our set of seven Stylish Mustaches on a card was a surprise success. To this day we're not sure why these cheap mustaches are such a hit. Is it the retro package? Is it the days of the week spin? We tried to capture the same feel with our spinoff mustache products, but none have managed to garner the same success.

## Catalog #62:

Change your mustache like you change your socks! This 7-piece collection of stylish mustaches allows you to have a dashing new look each day of the week. Monday you're the Hero, Thursday you're the Weasel. Made of life-like synthetic hair and backed with adhesive tape, these little lip-rugs can dramatically change your appearance, giving you a debonair and unpredictable appeal.

Pencil Thin Mustaches, 2005

# HAZARDOUS SNACKBOX

It seemed a natural idea, put the biohazard symbol on a lunchbox and sell it with the tag line, "No one will ever steal your lunch again!" It actually was funny in a pre-Homeland Security world, but a group of safety consultants (bureaucratic busybodies) didn't think so. When a hospital employee found one of these in the lunch room refrigerator, he went online and posted a comment on a safety discussion board that provoked a slew of furious responses. Think of the children using this snackbox and becoming desensitized to the biohazard symbol. Think of the children! They turned us in to the US Department of Transportation who informed us that it is against the law to put the biohazard symbol on any vessel that couldn't safely contain such material. At their request, we pulled it from the market. Failure to comply could have resulted in a $250,000 a day fine and possible criminal charges that carried the threat of a five year prison sentence. If you have one of these highly collectible snackboxes, please don't send it through the mail, leave it unattended in a public space or try to carry it on a plane. You have been warned.

Debuted 1998

FRONT

BACK

# MARTIAN POPPING THING

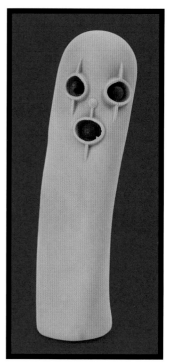

**MARTIAN CUKE**

The Martian Popping Thing is a Taiwanese designed baby toy that we renamed, put in custom packaging and sold as a stress reliever. Its counterpart was not as well-received despite our attempts to downplay its phallic nature by changing its color to green and calling it the Martian Cuke.

## Catalog #4:

It's baaaaaack! This is an actual likeness of a Martian citizen, with stress-reducing powers that are out of this world! Squeeze it and its eyes, ears and nose pop out. Watch your troubles and frustrations fly out the door when you make the creature's features bulge out of its head! The Martian Popping Thing™ could be your next best friend. This 4½" tall orange soft rubbery Martian has two blue eyes, two red ears, a red nose and a smiling mouth.

Debuted 1985

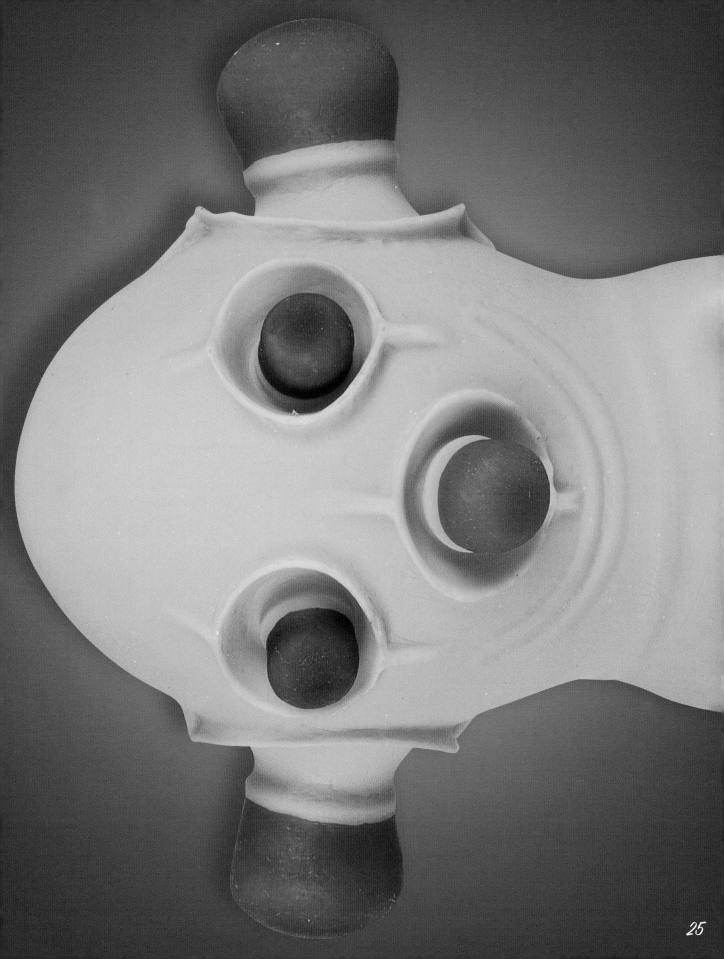

# EXCITED MONSTERS

**Debuted 1994**

These bizarre and beautiful rubber monsters were perfect for our line. We didn't even have to come up with a name for them since they came in a box with "Excited Monsters" printed right on the front. Were they designed by someone who had tapped into the primal fears deep within the collective psyche, or sketched out in a couple of minutes to meet a tight deadline? Either way, they're one of the most adorably terrifying products we've ever had the honor of selling.

## Catalog #34:

Never before has such a wide selection of tentacled, clawed, gaping-mouthed, bug-eyed monsters been available for purchase. They are 1½" to 3" long and made of rubber. Multicolored, glorious textures, many different but all bizarre.

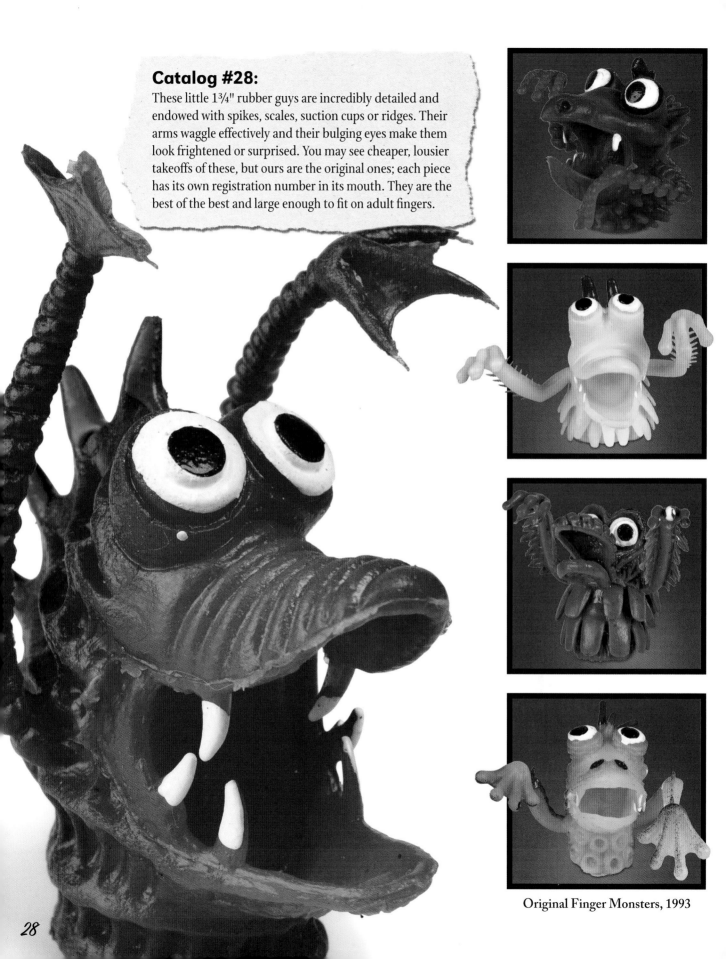

## Catalog #28:

These little 1¾" rubber guys are incredibly detailed and endowed with spikes, scales, suction cups or ridges. Their arms waggle effectively and their bulging eyes make them look frightened or surprised. You may see cheaper, lousier takeoffs of these, but ours are the original ones; each piece has its own registration number in its mouth. They are the best of the best and large enough to fit on adult fingers.

Original Finger Monsters, 1993

# FINGER MONSTERS

The original Deluxe Finger Monsters were masterpieces of simple design: scary, funny and absolutely irresistible. Over the years, the manufacturer allowed the molds to degrade and began using a cheaper grade of rubber. Rather than selling sub-par finger monsters, we bravely designed our own. We were careful to hold on to the charm of the originals while updating the look and color. It wasn't long before these achieved the same classic status as the originals.

Our Exclusive
Finger Monsters, 2003

29

# HULA GIRL

Producing our Hula Girl was more difficult than we thought it would be. The designer at the factory had probably never seen a Polynesian person and couldn't get the skin tone right. The first try was pumpkin orange and the next was bright yellow. They never did get the color right, but we loved the strangely bright Hula Girl so much that we decided to promote sexual equality amongst island novelties by producing the Hula Guy.

Debuted 1998

**HULA GUY**

## Catalog #58:

Turn your car into a tropical island on wheels by attaching these 7" hula dancers to your dashboard. Each ceramic dancer is dressed in a synthetic fiber "grass" skirt and strums a ukulele. The Hula Guy and Hula Girl are tireless dancers and will sway their hips to whatever music is on the radio. We even caught them doing their hula thing to the beat of an NPR commentary!

# SURFER BOB

We didn't design Surfer Bob, but we did give him his sublimely generic moniker. The response to his catalog debut was lukewarm, however, the minute he was removed from the catalog, customers began calling in to ask what happened to him. Eventually we decided to give him another chance and he sold much better than we anticipated. Based on his success we designed a spinoff product in the form of Surfer Betty. She wasn't nearly as popular as Bob, but rumor has it she was a better surfer.

**SURFER BETTY**

Debuted 1989

### Catalog #13:
Put this on your dashboard and watch the surfer action as your car weaves in and out of traffic. Or mount this on your computer to remind you of what other people are doing as your eyes are glued to the screen. As featured in *Earth Girls Are Easy*. Wave, board and surfer are about 4½" tall. Attach with self-adhesive foam tape.

# TIKI MUGS

Tiki Shot Glasses, 2003

## Catalog #67:

Now you can look cool even when you're drinking Kool Aid! A set of 4 highly sophisticated 5½" ceramic Tiki Mugs in all their collectible glory will give an edge of hip to even the lamest beverage. Perfect for everything from Hawaiian Punch to a Lime Ricky. Each set comes with 4 different mugs each with its own color and design.

Original Tiki Mugs, 2001

Sherm, Klaus, Carlos & Bela, 2004

Big Mouth Tiki Mugs, 2003

33

# PLASTIC HUT

T he fact that the packaging and contents of the Plastic Hut haven't changed since it was introduced over 50 years ago is a testament to its enduring appeal. Some customers of ours sold these on the web to raise money for the down payment on a house. Hopefully, when they moved in, it wasn't full of disproportionate animals and fencing.

Debuted 1994

### Catalog #31:

So much fun packed into a great box! Beautiful, full-color 40's style box opens to reveal tan-colored plastic hut. The roof, door and floor are detachable, and holy cow! Inside you'll find a barnyard bevy of fun! There are 5 pigs, 4 cows, 3 geese, 3 chickens, 3 bunnies and 3 farmyard folk to keep track of them all. But wait, this farm set even gives you 8 sections of fence to build your own corral, then rebuild it if the pigs get rambunctious and knock down the walls. There's even a pig trough to keep them distracted while you rebuild. Not all figures are to scale, or the bunnies would be very scary, since they're about as big as Ma and Pa! Still, it's a lot of farm fun for the price, especially with its great box!

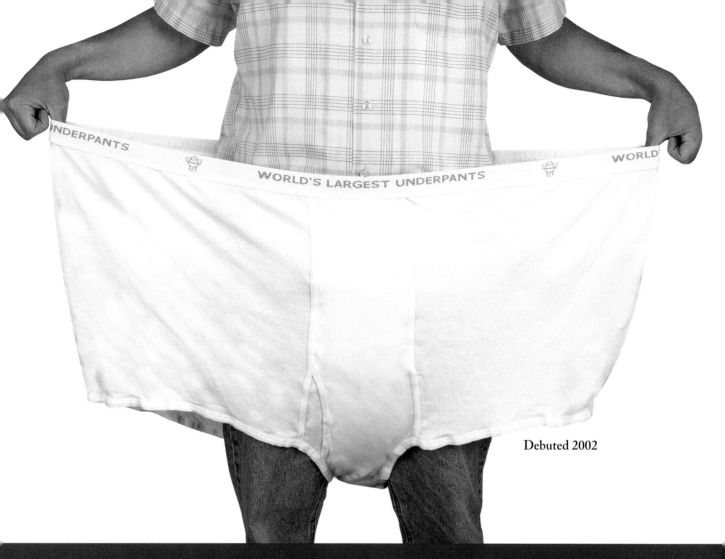

WORLD'S LARGEST UNDERPANTS

Debuted 2002

# GIANT UNDERPANTS

The rules of comedy are very clear, regular underpants are funny, but the World's Largest Underpants are REALLY funny. Inspired by the giant boxer shorts that came with membership in the Pee Wee Herman Fan Club, we decided to make the largest underpants ever mass-produced. Because the US government views our underpants as a threat to domestic giant underpants production (of which there is none) we have to pay special taxes and buy quota rights to import these.

### Catalog #68:
These 100% cotton, size 98-100 underpants stretch the definition of briefs. Each high-quality undergarment has a convenient double flap in the front and a sturdy elastic band to fit around the waist for maximum comfort. They come in the traditional white only and will shrink a bit after washing.

# RUBBER COCKROACH

The humor of a rubber cockroach is universal, transcending language, culture and status. Through the years we've sold many different styles in all sorts of quantities (including 144 in a "gross" bag), but we're most proud of the fine detail and craftsmanship of our Giant Deluxe Cockroach.

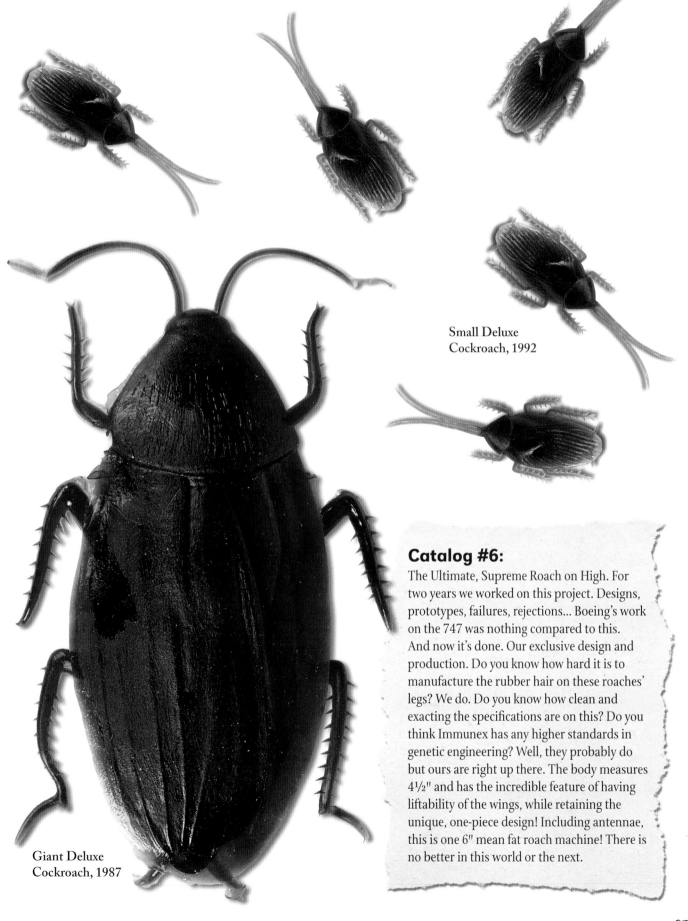

Small Deluxe
Cockroach, 1992

Giant Deluxe
Cockroach, 1987

## Catalog #6:

The Ultimate, Supreme Roach on High. For two years we worked on this project. Designs, prototypes, failures, rejections... Boeing's work on the 747 was nothing compared to this. And now it's done. Our exclusive design and production. Do you know how hard it is to manufacture the rubber hair on these roaches' legs? We do. Do you know how clean and exacting the specifications are on this? Do you think Immunex has any higher standards in genetic engineering? Well, they probably do but ours are right up there. The body measures 4½" and has the incredible feature of having liftability of the wings, while retaining the unique, one-piece design! Including antennae, this is one 6" mean fat roach machine! There is no better in this world or the next.

# SEÑOR MISTERIOSO

$W$hile the back of the package suggested a fake mysterious history for Señor Misterioso, he does have a secret. Our shadowy señor is actually an almost canonized Catholic Saint from Venezuela named Jose Gregorio Hernandez — a medical doctor who spent his life caring for the poor. Since he was mostly unknown to people outside of Venezuela, we reinvented him as a mysterious looming figure with a conspiratorial past and a glow-in-the-dark suit. One popular use for Señor Misterioso is to take pictures of him at odd locations and post them online. The myth of Misterioso lives on!

Debuted 2000

Debuted 1993

# PUNCHING NUN

A natural outgrowth of Punch and Judy puppets, the Punching Puppet mechanism makes punching as simple as pressing a lever. Our Punching Nun Puppet is a gentle tweak on a familiar holy figure. Before our pious pugilistic puppet, the mechanism was used mostly to advertise movies and politicians. In fact, the secret of our Punching Nun Puppet is that her head is actually a Margaret Thatcher sculpt left over from one of her election campaigns. Instead of making a new mold, we just added a habit and transformed the Iron Lady of the United Kingdom into the holy lady of Catholic primary schools.

**MARGARET THATCHER**

# DEVIL DUCKIE

We created the Devil Duckie as an alternative to the cheery and ubiquitous rubber ducky. But we had no idea that our little horned bath toy would take the country by storm, showing up in advertising campaigns, celebrity photo shoots, television shows and movies. In fact, the Devil Duckie has become a symbol of our company and continues to be one of our top sellers every year.

Original Devil Duckie, 2000

## Catalog #66:

Nothing is sweeter or more innocent than a rubber duckie, right? Wrong. This little, 4½" long, rubber Devil Duckie is one sinful squeaker. You'll think you're soaking in the hot magma pools of Hades when he leers at you with his arched eyebrow in your evening bath. He may be a representative of the dark side, but it's hard to resist his tiny horns and cute, chubby red body. Includes lyrics to the Devil Duckie theme song!

Hot Rod, 2003

Tattoo, 2006

Zombie, 2007

# NERD GLASSES

Debuted 1995

In the mid-1990s there was a huge shift in how the word "nerd" was used. As the importance of computers and the internet increased, so did the status of the people that understood them. What once was a term of derision became a badge of honor. Our Nerd Glasses were the first product to recognize this shift. The glasses themselves have been around forever, but instead of selling them as a way to make fun of nerds, we sold them as a visible beacon of your nerdy status. We wear them with pride.

# DISGUISE GLASSES

Debuted 1985

These Disguise Glasses have become a universal indicator of silliness. We sold them individually and also in a party pack of twelve. Why would people need that many? Group photographs. They have been worn by entire graduating classes, the board of directors at multinational companies and even for family reunions where the family is a little bit different. There is even a rumor that one of our customers asked that they be worn at his funeral because it would be impossible to mourn while wearing them.

Our Exclusive
Voodoo Doll, 1987

# VOODOO DOLL

The Voodoo Doll is part of Louisiana's voodoo tradition, but there are two versions. The first is a "real" doll that uses clothing or hair from the victim to create sympathetic magic that will cause them physical harm. The second is the easier to understand, dumbed-down tourist doll that you can put on your mantle to scare your neighbors. We originally sold one of these simplified versions with all of the magic literally written on the doll and thought, what if instead of the simple physical ailments we used actual modern problems and annoyances? For our exclusive Voodoo Doll we gave people the option of using voodoo for everything from headaches and parking tickets to true love and promotions. Believe it or not, we have actually had one returned because it didn't work.

## Catalog #7:

At last, our exclusive Voodoo Doll is in stock. We had an entire village in China hand sew these beauties. Why voodoo? It's the now thing RIGHT NOW. For once in your life you can be the first on your block to own one before you see it on TV, read about it in USA Today or see the oddball feature story on the lower left side of the second section of the Wall Street Journal. It is 9" tall of stuffed bright red fabric. The header color is Haitian yellow with the words: IS IT VOODOO? Printed in aqua blue. On the reverse are the instructions: "We think you know what to do with this. And we hope that you only use the white pins. However, since you have free choice in life, we have supplied the black pins as well." How many times have you searched the city for a reasonably priced voodoo doll? Your search is over. No special training is required. This is not a toy so please do not give to children or nut cases. And don't be messing with the voodoo world if you are silly.

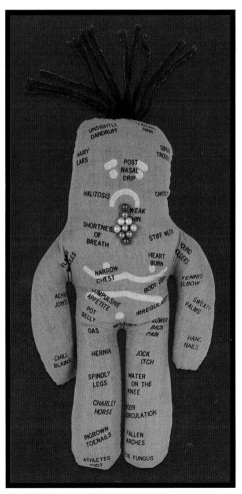

Original Voodoo Doll, 1986

The first catapult gun, the Bug Gun, was not a great success. During that time we also sold tiny pigs that fit neatly in the trough of the catapult, in fact, the pigs were a better fit than the insects. After tossing pigs around the office for weeks, we decided we had to sell a Pig Catapult. This was such a hit that others quickly followed. Since the names of these catapult guns are so essential to their success, we often come up with the name before the product is actually designed.

# CATAPULT GUNS

### Catalog #21:

This is a 5¾" bug flinger, with medieval catapult action! Just like the ones used from 360 B.C. to 400 A.D. during siege warfare throughout the world! Now you can safely fling soft rubber bugs and reptiles at your friends and relatives while demonstrating this important physical mechanism!

Debuted 1991

# BENDY MONSTERS

## Catalog #39:

Have you ever wondered what mythological creatures did in the '70s? Wonder no more: they formed a disco band and went on tour. All of these monsters are brightly colored, 5" long, made of bendable rubber, and mellow enough to be bent into almost any position. Medusa is wearing bell-bottoms and a tank top, while Caliban has borrowed his look from Elton John with big eyes that look like glasses and a web under his arms that looks like a cape. The rest of the gang includes Cerberus, Hydra, Sphinx and King Kong. They'll make you feel like dancing!

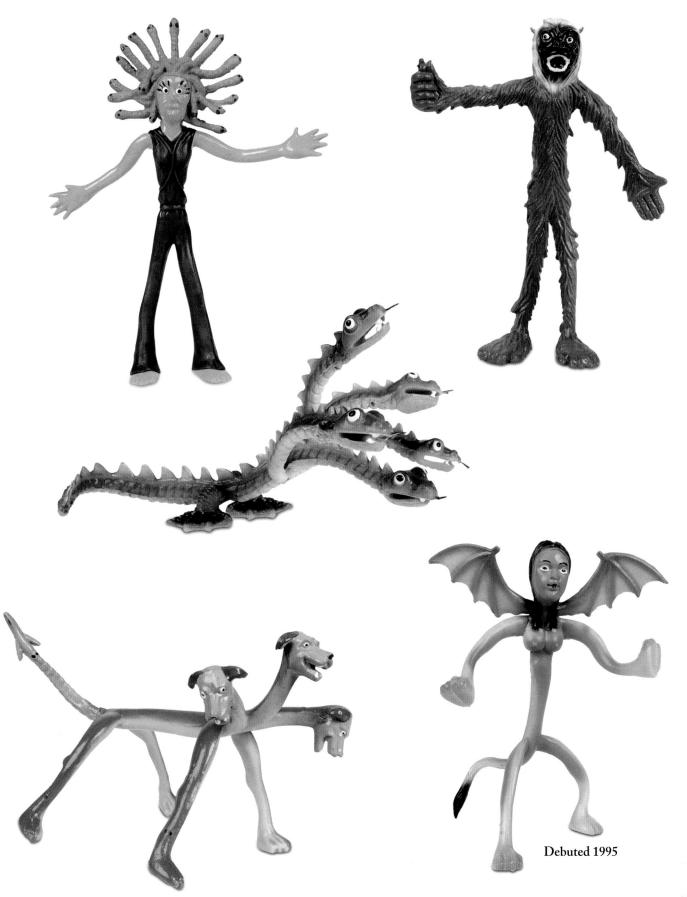

Debuted 1995

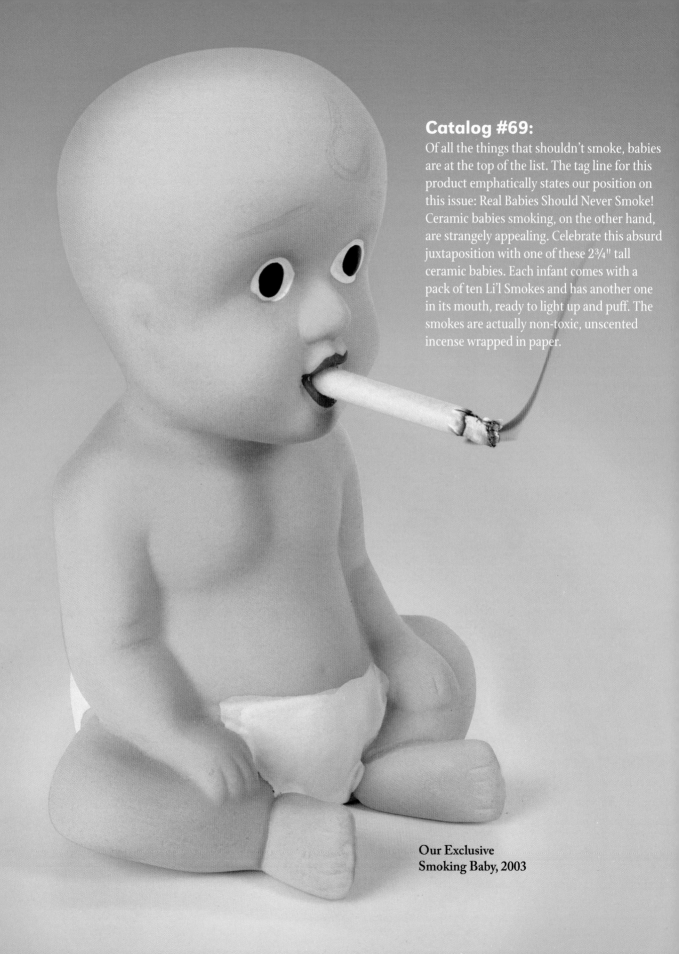

## Catalog #69:

Of all the things that shouldn't smoke, babies are at the top of the list. The tag line for this product emphatically states our position on this issue: Real Babies Should Never Smoke! Ceramic babies smoking, on the other hand, are strangely appealing. Celebrate this absurd juxtaposition with one of these 2¾" tall ceramic babies. Each infant comes with a pack of ten Li'l Smokes and has another one in its mouth, ready to light up and puff. The smokes are actually non-toxic, unscented incense wrapped in paper.

**Our Exclusive
Smoking Baby, 2003**

# SMOKING BABY

$B$ack when smoking was considered acceptable, the Smoking Baby was a common novelty for kids. The original version was a simple, crudely sculpted plastic figure with a tiny hole to hold the cigarette. But no one really cared about the baby, the magic was in the cigarette. These tiny miracles contained "puff puff" technology that made it appear as if the baby was puffing clouds and rings as it smoked instead of just emitting a steady stream. When we inquired about making our own version we discovered that "puff puff" technology had disappeared. There were no factories that remembered how to make the cigarettes. We spent months making inquiries, but were rebuffed at every turn. We even sent over a few precious samples of the original cigarettes from our private collection to be analyzed and were told that they contained substances that couldn't be identified. So, while our new version looks a lot better than the original, we had to settle for smokes made of incense, which are sadly lacking any "puff puff" magic.

**"PUFF PUFF" TECHNOLOGY**

Even without the fancy cigarettes our customers loved the product, however, Marlboro® cigarettes threatened to sue us. They contended we were encouraging young people, and babies, to smoke and because our package of mini incense cigarettes vaguely resembled their packaging, they would be blamed for it.

Original Smoking Baby, 1991

Debuted 2002

# DONKEY CIGARETTE DISPENSER

**Catalog #68:**

You smoke (even though you probably shouldn't) and being the suave smoker you are, you want the latest in smoking accessories. Store your favorite smokes in this donkey's pack and when you need a fix, just press his ears down and he'll dispense a cigarette from his behind. Each 7½" long by 5" tall plastic burro is a charmingly crude addition to any room.

There have been novelty cigarette dispensers since mass-production standardized cigarette sizes. Our Donkey Cigarette Dispenser is a fresh take on a classic design that has existed for about a century. Even though the popularity of smoking has decreased, it continues to be popular. Probably because non-smokers think it's funny to watch a smoker pull a cigarette from an ass. The Ellen DeGeneres show featured a Donkey Cigarette Dispenser as a prop which made it popular as an objet d'art completely divorced from any practical use it might have.

# SURPLUS

Surplus items have always been one of the cornerstones of our business. As wonderful as it is to create something strange, it's even more wonderful to find it. Many of these items come from the humorless, utilitarian world of the military where function trumps form. Take for instance the Urine Specimen Jar. In its original setting you probably wouldn't even notice it, but put one on your desk with a few pens in it and you've got a conversation piece.

Sometimes we don't find the stuff, the stuff finds us. We've had people approach us with truckloads of weird stuff at bargain prices because they know we're up to the challenge of marketing it.

The surplus market is always a crapshoot, but for every dud, there's an amazing discovery. So, we're always on the lookout for interesting objects to resurrect, repurpose and recycle. It's these products that have made the Archie McPhee catalog one of the strangest and most unpredictable publications to ever show up in your mailbox.

# PORCELAIN HAND

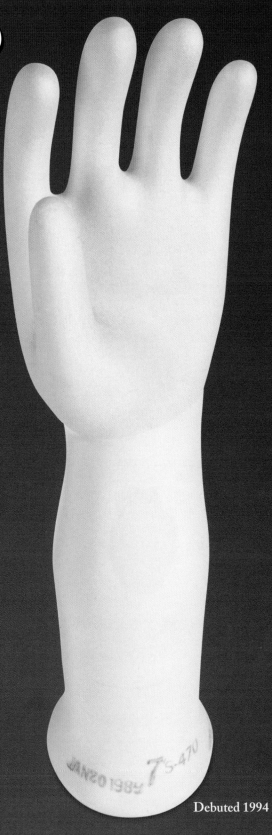

Of course, no one who bought the porcelain hand actually used it as a glove mold. In fact, it seemed to be an artistic inspiration. We have seen the hands incorporated into sculptures, parade floats and art installations. There is even a garden in Seattle with an entire pathway made from broken shards of the porcelain hands. When we received the hands they were tightly bolted onto steel beams. It took a lot of effort to work them loose and then clean them, which made porcelain hand preparation one of the least desirable jobs in the company.

**Catalog #31:**
These terrific, heavy porcelain hands were once used in the manufacture of gloves. Another one of Mark's fabulous finds, this time in Canada. We've said it before, he spans the globe and crosses any borders for these wonderful discoveries. Over 13 inches high and weighing more than 2 pounds, in various shapes and sizes. We had another load of these, and they went fast! Don't miss out on this batch. When they're gone, they're really gone!

Debuted 1994

# GLASS URINE CONTAINERS

Our customers generally aren't looking for poo related toys. The classic Whoopie Cushion is a little inelegant for the highbrow tastes of our clientele, but for some reason they have accepted urine into their collective heart. The popularity of the Urine Specimen Jar & Urinal Pitcher led directly to Pee Guy (page 171). For us, urine will always be number one.

(page 171)

Urinal Pitcher, 1997

Urine Specimen
Jar, 1994

## Catalog #46:

Need a classic vessel to hold pens, pipes, or paper clips? You're in luck! These thick glass flasks hold 175cc of almost any substance you need to store. Say you're into chemistry or you're into flower arranging. No problem. Or maybe you're in a bind and need a gift. This bottle is the perfect choice. It stands 5" tall and states in clear proud letters Perfection Urine Specimen Bottle. Display it proudly and everyone will suspect you're "in the know."

# DUMMY BOMB

## Catalog #4:

These were made during World War II at an exorbitant price paid by the taxpayers. They stand 35" tall. They are made out of lovely maple or oak! Each one weighs in at 25 lbs! They are 4½" in diameter at the base, 3½" at the midbody and tapering to a 3" diameter head. The flange and the base are steel, as well as near the tip. We suppose it was to simulate the weight and feel of a real bomb so the sailor/soldier cannon loaders could practice handling. Great for window displays, and possibly for making into a lamp. It is a work of art that cost the taxpayers $200 in 1944 (the shells are dated at the base). That is over $1000 in current value dollars. What a thoughtful gift one of these would make. We plan to drop a few of them onto certain people who have given us rubber checks. Very limited stock, order today because once these are gone they are gone forever.

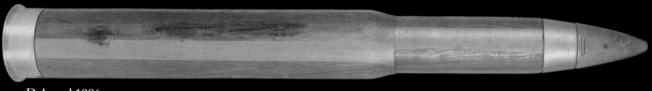

Debuted 1986

# 1960's FALLOUT SHELTER SIGN

## Catalog #32:

Some say the cold war is over, but you can keep it alive and well when you hang our "Fallout" sign on your front door. You and your neighbors will be secure in knowing exactly where to go when the big one drops. Ours is the original heavy-duty, 10" x 14" metal sign printed with reflective yellow ink over a matte, black background. There are four pre-drilled holes in the corners for easy installation. Once you put this sign up, it won't go anywhere. Don't delay — your life could depend on it!

FALLOUT SHELTER

Debuted 1994

# DUMMY U.S. NAVY TORPEDO

**BUSTED!**

When we purchased a pallet of dummy torpedoes from the University of Washington Physics Department auction all we could think about was how cool they would look mounted on top of a car or hanging over a pool table. They never had actual explosives inside them and there was no danger of them being used for any military purpose because the insides had all rusted and rotted away into an orange dust. They sold well enough that we were looking around for more when we got a visit from a representative of the Department of Defense Intelligence Unit. He showed up in a smart business suit that subtly revealed a firearm hanging from a shoulder holster and informed us that the torpedoes contained a guidance system that was still classified as Top Secret. It turned out, that despite being over 20 years old, they were still more advanced than what some enemies of the U.S. were using. He politely insisted that we retrieve them from our customers — immediately.

We contacted all the customers and had them ship the torpedoes back to us (with a full refund of course). Most people responded immediately, but there was one exception. One customer refused to answer our calls and letters. Soon we were visited by another DOD representative, this time decked out in a black suit and sunglasses. He asked that we provide him with all the contact information we had for the customer. We complied.

The next day, we got a call from that customer. He told us that a man in a black suit had shown up at his door a couple of hours after we turned over his address. The man introduced himself, walked immediately to where the torpedo was hanging in the house and took it down. The customer was freaked out because they had obviously been watching him and they knew where the torpedo was in the house even though it wasn't visible from a window. Then, he asked if he could still get a refund. We figured it was the least we could do.

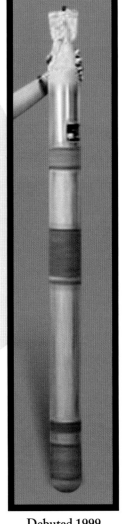

**Debuted 1999**

# DIKKENS

Dikkens came to us from a customer. She was cleaning out a relative's house and happened upon a few cases of them tucked away in the attic. What do you do when you happen across several hundred retro plastic and plush devils? You call Archie McPhee. We purchased all of them and became the exclusive distributor of the Dikkens doll thirty-three years after it was produced.

Debuted 2001

**Website:**

These original Kamar Dikkens dolls are 7" tall (sitting) with plastic heads, red felt bodies and bendable tails. They were actually made in Japan, which is very rare for a toy from 1968. The tag is just as good as the toy, one side says "Another wild thing by the Doll King." The other side says "My name is Dikkens, I am made of love."

# RECIPE CARDS

CASEROLES | Frankfurter Crown | CARD 84

© 1973 Curtin Publications, Inc., New York, N.Y.

WEIGHT CONTROL | Tomato Aspic with Shrimp | CARD 126

PRINTED IN U.S.A.

CASSEROLES | Macaroni, Ham & Cheese Bake | CARD 81

© 1973 Curtin Publications, Inc., New York, N.Y.

PRINTED IN U.S.A.

Debuted 1995

## Catalog #40:

The year was 1973. Nixon was president, the Carpenters were at their peak, Dad was wearing baby-blue leisure suits and Mom just might have used these cards to whip up dinner. Photographed in the earth tones of the '70s, but with the saturated colors (and fats) of the '50s, these earnest "Kitchen Tested Recipes" include calorie counts, average preparation time, and even menu suggestions — after all, what good is a Ground Beef Muffin Melt without peppermint-stick ice cream? You get all 180 in the Complete Family Recipe Card Library, so take those giant wooden forks off your wall and serve up some Waldorf Salad just like Mom used to make.

# HE SHE DOLLS

The He She dolls were actual factory mistakes from a line of action figures based on the semi-popular cartoon series about a 1980's pop band, called Jem. They accidently put Jem's boyfriend Rio's head on Jem's body and then gave him/her Jem's makeup and hair. They were so alluring and disturbing that we couldn't keep them in stock. When we sold the last one we asked the factory to repeat the mistake. As you might expect, the intentional mistake was not as cool as the original. Instead of the male head on female bodies, they just sent us an effeminate male action figure in female clothes.

**AMAZING ORIGINAL**

**INFERIOR REMAKE**

Debuted 1992

### Catalog #22:
We can't believe how lucky we are to have these. Imagine our delight when we discovered a whole box of Barbie® type dolls in high fashion female outfits. But with male heads! It's about time cross-dressers had a representative toy! These are great, one-of-a-kind, one-shot deals, and you need one.

# CAMPUS CUTIES

## Catalog #34:

We thought of renaming these "Potential Monster
Movie Victims" because they all seem so unsuspect-
ing and most are scantily clad. They really don't look
like anyone we went to college with, but most of us
went to alternative colleges that didn't have the Greek
system, and these are *definitely* sorority girls. Eight
different, in assorted poses and campus wear. 6" tall
and made of bone-colored plastic.

Debuted 1994

# SHREDDED MONEY

The moment we found out that the United States Treasury Department sold strips of shredded currency we knew our customers would want it. Other companies were selling it in boring ways — sealed in plastic pens and keychains. We were going to sell it in giant bales and gallon jugs for whatever purpose our customers wanted!

In fact, we suggested that customers try to glue it back together or use it as packing material or kindling to start a fire. Soon after we received our first orders we were contacted by the Secret Service and told that we were not allowed to sell it unless it was in a permanently sealed container. They also told us that we couldn't sell it as kindling, packing material or with the implication that customers could glue it back together and make new money. Oops.

We continued to try and sell this for several years sealed in thick, United States Treasury Department approved, plastic bags but it sold slowly. As it sat in the warehouse, we discovered another negative about Shredded Money, it smells terrible. To handle the money we had to wear plastic gloves and face masks. Even then, the odor was overwhelming. Our desire to remove it from the warehouse was so great that we considered cutting our losses by taking it all to the dump, but soon discovered that according to the Environmental Protection Agency, it is forbidden to put shredded money in a landfill because of potential danger to the environment. It was impossible to get rid of.

Eventually we sold the whole lot of it back to the guy we bought it from at a huge loss. Yes, we actually lost money selling money.

**Debuted 1996**

BUSTED!

# SWEDISH EAR SYRINGE

**Website:**
Almost too lovely to believe! This 9½" metal syringe can help you keep those ear canals free of excessive ear wax. A couple squirts while you are in the shower and you'll be feeling fresh and clean. Mother will be proud! Plus, you'll be hearing everything loud and clear. Comes with two tips, one rounded, one straight. Note: This is sold as a novelty item only. Clean your ears at your own risk.

Debuted 2003

# HOWDY DOODY KEYCHAIN

I picked up the Howdy Doody Puzzle Keychain in the mid-80s after discovering it in Jerry "King of New Jersey Novelties" Pressner's Brooklyn warehouse. However, I didn't get the complete carded products that were sold at stores, I got large bags of plastic pieces that had to be assembled. Even though it came with pads of instructions, assembling hundreds of them was a mind-numbing job. In fact, we still have boxes of unassembled pieces we never got around to putting together.

**DISASSEMBLED**

### Catalog #1:
Original "Howdy Doody" from the 1950s. 3½" plastic figure is actually a puzzle, held together by an "NBC" microphone. Original printed instruction card included. Obviously limited stock.

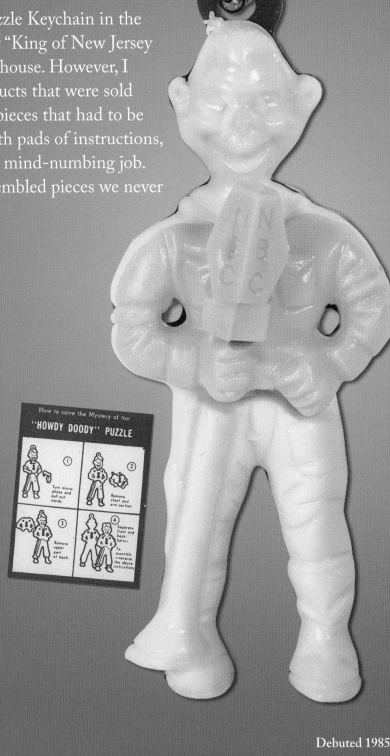

Debuted 1985

# HOKIE POKIE SOUND MACHINE

The Hokie Pokie Sound Machine was one of the worst devices ever invented for playing vinyl records. The sound quality from the tiny speaker was terrible and sometimes the truck would veer off course, causing the needle to carve a large scratch in the vinyl. We pointed this out in the description of the product, but that didn't stop people from buying them. They were so popular, in fact, that we still get requests for them to this day.

Debuted 1996

### Catalog #45:

Dust off that vinyl and put on your white dancin' shoes, 'cause the Hokie Pokie Sound Machine is rollin' into town. Very carefully align the needle in the groove, pull the lever and then start groovin'. Watch and listen as this light blue, 4½" x 2" plastic vehicle cruises your LP like a tiny ice cream truck, flashing its headlights and playing your favorite tunes. (Actually it plays the tunes on the LP, whether they're your favorites or not). You could use this on your collectible albums; however, they may not be so collectible afterwards. Comes with two "Hokie Pokie" decals and requires a 9-volt battery (not included).

**NEEDLE AND GUIDING WHEEL**

# GI MAN HEADS

Near our corporate headquarters, there's a company that produces replacement parts for classic action figures. This company found themselves with too many heads and asked if we wanted a couple thousand of them. When they first appeared on our website, we got a letter of complaint about them saying, "It's unconscionable that you would sell a bag of military action figure heads while our men and women are dying overseas." They never explained exactly why that was so.

**Website:**

Let's make a deal. You don't ask us why we're selling these and we won't ask you why you're buying them. It's a set of 20 assorted GI Joe heads with a hole in the bottom where their body should be. Each is about 2" tall with varied features and hairstyles, from fascist buzz cut to Village People mustache. We're sure you'll think of a million things to do with these like... well... you know.

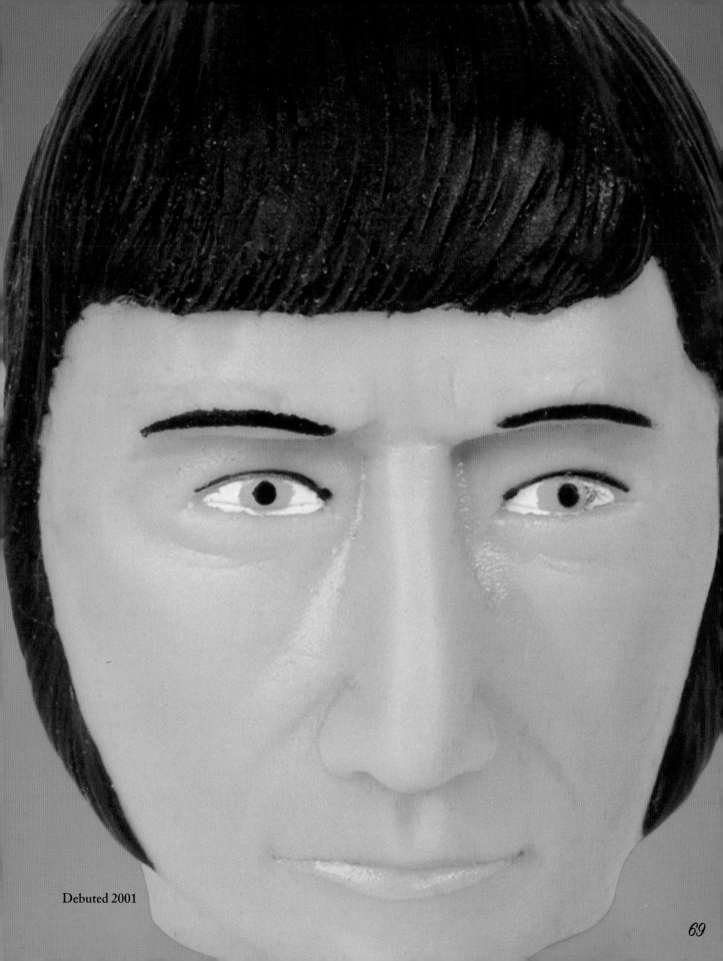

Debuted 2001

69

# GO FIGURE

The phrase "action figure" was invented by Hasbro® as a way to sell dolls to young boys. Since that time the market for action figures has changed. What used to be an industry exclusively for children has been taken over by adult collectors and super fans. Since most action figures are based on television, movie and comic book characters, we decided to ignore the typical subjects and make action figures of important historical figures and under-appreciated people from everyday life. In other words, we are using the phrase to sell dolls to smart adults.

We started with Jesus and then chose a wide range of artists, authors, composers and the like to round out our line of historical action figures. The "regular people" line of figures started with a barista, but now includes many others like a male nurse and a lunch lady.

But this section is not limited to just action figures. We've also sold the classic bobbing head dolls, miniature articulated figures, and, most recently, groups of figures that come packaged together in a play set.

We hope that our figures represent the real heroes and characters that populate your life. Surely your local librarian made more of a difference in your life than Cobra Commander or a Transformer. If not, the Freud Action Figure makes an excellent gift for your therapist.

# LIBRARIAN
## ACTION FIGURE

It started as a joke Nancy Pearl made at a dinner party. Who would ever make an action figure of a librarian? Well, we did and it has become a best seller and a national phenomenon. The model for the action figure, Nancy Pearl, is an amazing person with boundless energy, humor and enthusiasm for reading. She is everything a librarian should be. However, some librarians felt that this action figure represented negative stereotypes about their profession and took their concerns to the media. They complained that the action figure made them look like dowdy, humorless, older women who shush people and take themselves too seriously. Jack Broom of the Seattle Times wrote an article about their dissatisfaction. This resulted in enormous media attention and the controversy was featured in hundreds of newspapers, Time Magazine, Reader's Digest and even made the cover of the "Daily Times" newspaper in Pakistan in the midst of their nuclear standoff with India.

In an effort to make the discontented minority happy, we produced a deluxe version of the action figure with brighter clothing, a book cart and a reference desk with computer terminal. Of course, they weren't satisfied with the deluxe version either, proving that there are at least a few humorless librarians who take themselves too seriously.

### LIBRARIAN
#### ACTION FIGURE
##### TRADING CARD

**Name:** Nancy Pearl  **Occupation:** Librarian
**Weapon of Choice:** The Dewey Decimal System
**Mission:** To promote and celebrate the written word.
**Accomplishments:** Director of Library Programming and the Washington Center for the Book at the Seattle Public Library. Nancy is best known for the "If All Seattle Read The Same Book" project. This idea of one city reading the same book at the same time has been imitated in cities around the world. She is a book reviewer for the Seattle Times, Booklist, Library Journal, KUOW-FM Seattle, and KWGS-FM Tulsa. Avid bicyclist who has twice completed the Seattle to Portland Bicycle Classic.
**Awards:** 2003 Washington Humanities Award, 2001 Allie Beth Martin Award from the American Library Association, 1998 Library Journal's Fiction Reviewer of the Year.
**Education:** Masters Degree in Library Science from the University of Michigan.
**Interesting Fact:** Decided to become a librarian at the age of 10.
**Books Written:** Book Lust: Recommended Reading for Every Mood, Moment, and Reason; Now Read This: A Guide to Mainstream Fiction, 1978–1998; and Now Read This II: A Guide to Mainstream Fiction, 1990–2001.
**Favorite Books:** Fiction—The Brothers K, The Prince of Tides, Searching for Caleb, The Eyre Affair, A Gay and Melancholy Sound. Non-Fiction—The Best and the Brightest, Love Thy Neighbor: A Story of War, Train Go Sorry: Inside a Deaf World, The Liars' Club, Into Thin Air.
©ACCOUTREMENTS

**AMAZING SHUSHING ACTION**

## Catalog #70:

You can have all the books, magazines, periodicals, journals, videos, and CD ROMs in the world, but without a librarian you'll be frustrated and overwhelmed before you can say "Dewey Decimal System." And although most librarians can't travel faster than a speeding bullet, or leap over tall buildings in a single bound, they can direct you to an article on the physics of speed, an instructional pamphlet on high jumping, and a book of photographs of the world's tallest buildings. Each 5" tall, hard plastic Librarian Action Figure is modeled after Nancy Pearl, a real-life librarian in the Seattle area. Press the button on her back and her arm will move with amazing "shushing action!" Comes with a tiny plastic replica of her most recent book, Book Lust, and a stack of random literature.

Debuted 2003

# Dick, the ALBINO BOWLER
## ACTION FIGURE

**REALISTIC BOWLING ACTION**

Debuted 2002

## Catalog #68:

The doors swing wide open and he stands in the doorway — a pale figure with stark white hair and a bowling bag. It's Dick, the Albino Bowler, and he's come to bowl. If you're lucky enough to be at one of the small town bowling alleys he chooses to visit, you're in for a treat. Soon everyone in the alley will be gathered around his lane to witness his extraordinary display of bowling virtuosity and his thick white sideburns. Each 5" tall action figure is made of hard plastic and comes with his traditional white ball. Push the button on his back and he'll send the ball down the lane!

## Catalog #71:

They're big, they're hairy, and they're notoriously elusive! This 7¼" tall, hard plastic Bigfoot Action Figure has stamps on the bottom of its feet and comes with a stamp pad so you can leave mysterious footprints on letters, walls and skin. Intricate articulation allows it to be posed just like frame 352 of the famous film footage.

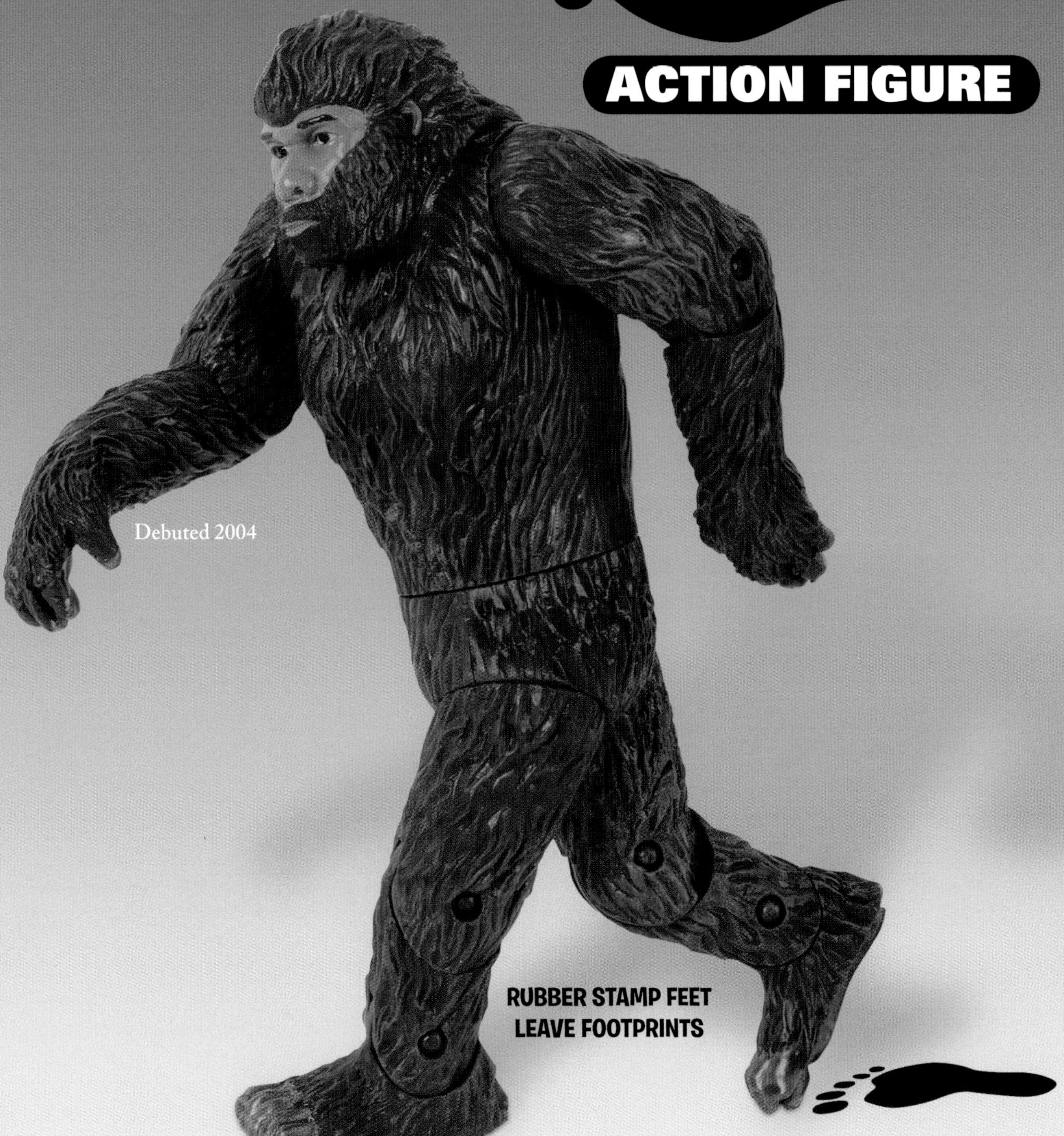

# BIGFOOT
## ACTION FIGURE

Debuted 2004

**RUBBER STAMP FEET
LEAVE FOOTPRINTS**

# LUNCH LADY
## ACTION FIGURE

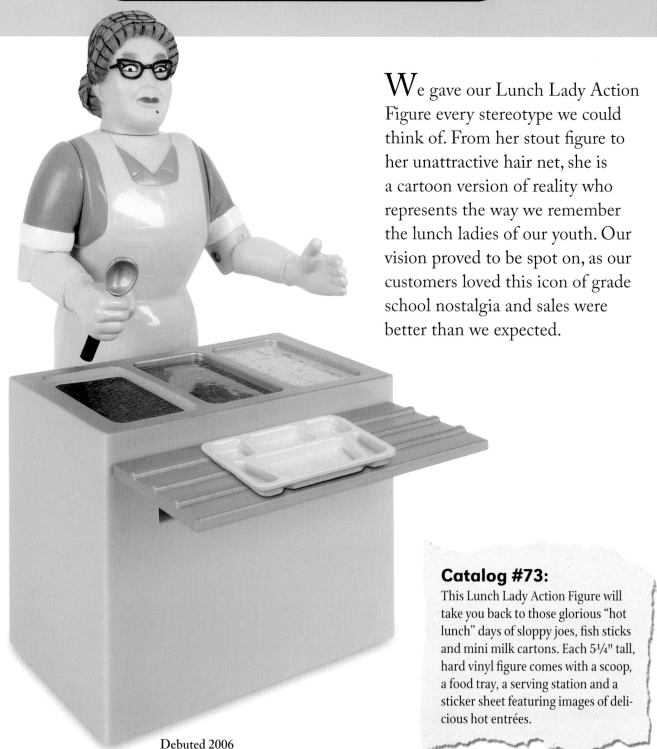

We gave our Lunch Lady Action Figure every stereotype we could think of. From her stout figure to her unattractive hair net, she is a cartoon version of reality who represents the way we remember the lunch ladies of our youth. Our vision proved to be spot on, as our customers loved this icon of grade school nostalgia and sales were better than we expected.

**Catalog #73:**
This Lunch Lady Action Figure will take you back to those glorious "hot lunch" days of sloppy joes, fish sticks and mini milk cartons. Each 5¼" tall, hard vinyl figure comes with a scoop, a food tray, a serving station and a sticker sheet featuring images of delicious hot entrées.

Debuted 2006

# CRAZY CAT LADY
## ACTION FIGURE

**Catalog #71:**
Every town has a Crazy Cat Lady. She's the one who lives in a tiny house full of feral felines. This 5¼" tall, hard vinyl Crazy Cat Lady Action Figure has a wild look in her eye and comes with six cats.

Debuted 2004

# MARIE ANTOINETTE
## ACTION FIGURE

**Catalog #73:**

Marie Antoinette's reign as the Queen of France was clouded in controversy. Her extravagant lifestyle led many to believe that she was not worthy of the throne and eventually she became widely despised as the epitome of incompetence and frivolity within the French royalty. During the French Revolution, Marie was stripped of her crown, imprisoned and beheaded by guillotine in front of a cheering crowd. This 5½" tall, hard vinyl figure features amazing "Ejector Head Action," and comes with a removable plastic wig and dress.

**EJECTOR HEAD**

Debuted 2006

# SIGMUND FREUD
## ACTION FIGURE

### Catalog #68:

Celebrate the great achievements of the man responsible for modern psychotherapy with this Sigmund Freud Action Figure. Each 5" tall figure captures Freud in a pensive pose, holding a distinctly phallic cigar. Prop him on your desk or nightstand to inspire you to explore the depths of your unconscious and embrace the symbolism of your dreams.

Debuted 2002

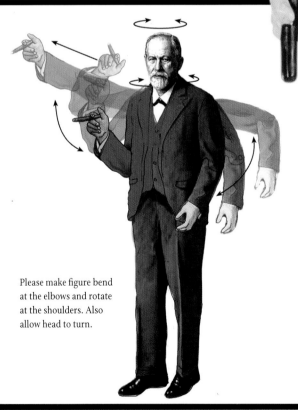

Please make figure bend at the elbows and rotate at the shoulders. Also allow head to turn.

Original Design Sketch, 2001

# FUZZ
## ACTION FIGURE
### HIPSTER · PHILOSOPHER · CYNIC

**THE REAL FUZZ**

People generally buy action figures of their heroes, but would they buy one of just an average, unknown guy? We decided to answer this question by making an action figure of one of our employees. We chose Craig "Fuzz" Garrett, a popular figure in the office and a man with a colorful nickname. With his cooperation, the Fuzz Action Figure was born. The final figure looked remarkably like Craig and we even included two extra heads to reflect his ever changing hairstyles. The initial response was encouraging, but we found that most people had trouble believing that Fuzz was really just a guy who worked in our office and eventually sales dwindled off.

When we made the figure, Fuzz was single, smoked cigarettes, drank vodka martinis and lived at his parent's house. Today, Fuzz has a girlfriend, no longer smokes, prefers drinking local microbrews and *still* lives with his parents.

## Catalog #68:

The first thing you have to understand is that Fuzz is a real person. He's 21 years old, he lives with his parents and he just happens to have his own action figure. Each 5¾" representation of Fuzz in plastic form has moveable arms and legs and comes with three interchangeable heads! Match a head to one of Fuzz's personality traits, or pretend he's the victim of a cloning accident.

**INTERCHANGEABLE HEADS**

Debuted 2002

# HARRY HOUDINI
## ACTION FIGURE

The Houdini Action Figure presented a unique challenge for us. It was important that we show him escaping from something, but we had to decide if we should go with the more mainstream straightjacket and shackles, or something more unique? After all, Houdini escaped from many things, from a giant paper bag (without ripping it) to a locked mail sack. We were tempted to recreate his famous escape from inside of a sewn up squid, but unfortunately the logistics of including a giant squid proved to be too complex. Still, we're proud of the strange assortment of bondage accessories we included with this action figure. We think Houdini would approve.

### Catalog #72:

Harry Houdini was an accomplished magician and master of escape. His awe inspiring shows and death defying public performances earned him the title of "World's Greatest Escapologist!" This 5½" tall, hard vinyl action figure comes with all the classic tools of the trade: a cloth straight jacket, two sets of plastic shackles, a plastic chair and a bit of rope.

Debuted 2005

82

Debuted 2007

# FLESH EATING
# ZOMBIES

# HORRIFIED B-MOVIE VICTIMS

## Catalog #73:

We provide the victims, you provide the terror! Each dramatic play set includes nine 2½" to 3" tall, hard vinyl victims captured in utterly terrified poses! Are they reacting to the advances of a giant, man-eating alpaca or the sight of your grandma in her nightgown and curlers? The possibilities are endless!

## Catalog #74:

Wreak havoc on your sister's precious diorama with this Flesh Eating Zombie Play Set! Each set includes nine 1" to 3¼" tall, hard vinyl zombies, complete with blank stares, gaping mouths, open wounds and missing limbs! Turn off the lights and they glow! Fantastic undead fun for the whole family!

Debuted 2006

# THE CUBES

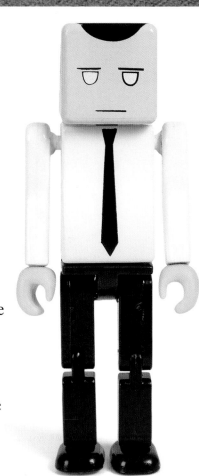

Realizing that many of our customers were buying our products to put in their cubicles at work, we set out to design the ultimate desk toy. We wanted to create something that captured the experience of working for a large, faceless corporation. After some research and brainstorming, we came up with The Cubes, miniature cubicle sets complete with a cube headed employee. The interactivity of setting up the cube walls, positioning the furniture and accessories, and decorating the walls proved to be a hit with all of the disillusioned people stuck in corporate jobs. We even extended the line to include a break room set and an IT set for all of the system administrators. It pleases us greatly to know that we've created an amusing distraction that has helped those stuck in tedious corporate jobs waste away countless hours on the company dime.

Bob Cube, 2004

Ann Cube, 2004

## Catalog #73:

Finally, the drudgery of corporate life has been captured in a play set for adults! Bob, Joe, Ted, and Ann spend eight hours a day, five days a week, at tiny desks in tiny cubicles in a giant room packed with countless similar cubicles in a giant building filled with countless similar rooms. Each set has one 2¾" tall posable plastic figure and all the necessary plastic parts to build a classic corporate cube: four walls, desk, chair, file cabinet, in/out box, phone, and computer. Build one to look exactly like your current workspace or, better yet, construct a whole labyrinth of cubes to make your own miniature office where you're the boss! Comes with a sticker sheet of decor for your cube, complete with graphs, charts, screens for the computer and pithy office posters. Also includes a job title sticker sheet so you can create a convoluted and meaningless position for your employee.

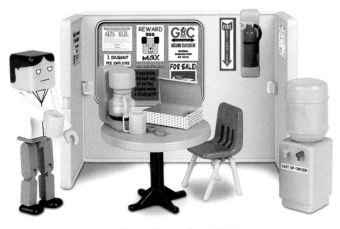

Break Room Set, 2005

IT Set, 2006

# LI'L SIDESHOW PLAY SETS

**Catalog #73:**

Step right up, Ladies and Gentlemen, and witness some of the strangest sights your eyes have ever seen! Behind this curtain you'll find some of nature's most amazing human beings! Watch in astonishment as the World's Strongest Man performs feats of human strength beyond your wildest imagination. Behold the enthralling Frog Girl and Lobster Boy, are they human or animal? Observe the stunning height difference between the World's Tallest Man and the World's Smallest Man, and don't forget to save time for our biggest surprise, a gal with the face of an angel and the beard of a pirate, the remarkable Bearded Lady! Each play set comes with a 5½" x 4" plastic stage and a 5¼" square vinyl banner featuring an old-time sideshow illustration.

**Debuted 2006**

# SHRINER NODDER

The image of a Shriner is deeply rooted in American pop culture. Archie McPhee has always had products based around some part of Shriner culture, most notably our line of fezzes, but this is our favorite. It was slightly smaller than our other nodders, but that was so it could fit in a tiny car.

### Catalog #69:

Take all the excitement of a tiny car and mix it with the fashion-forward statement of a fez and you've got yourself a Shriner. This 6¼" tall, tuxedoed Shriner Nodder embodies all the fun and fellowship of a real member of The Order!

Debuted 2003

# ROCK BAND

We bought these Rock Band Figures because they looked just like a generic rock band from the '60s. However, a member of a particular insect-named group thought it resembled he and his mop-topped companions a little too closely and issued a cease and desist order with a little help from his friends. It was not enough for us to simply stop selling them, we had to take pictures of them being crushed at the dump and the pieces scattering helter-skelter. Our initial response was to fight the lawsuit, but ultimately we decided to just let it be.

Dear Sir or Madame:

We represent Apple Corps Limited and the Apple Group of related companies ("Apple") which are wholly owned by Messrs. George Harrison, Paul McCartney and Richard Starkey and Ms. Yoko Ono Lennon, as Executrix of the Estate of John Lennon. Please be advised that Apple retains proprietary rights in the name and likenesses of The Beatles.

Debuted 1991

# THEMES

**P**eople approach us all the time with product ideas but we don't use any of them. We already have more ideas than we could ever produce.

We do, however, pay attention to what people like. Where are the trends going? What will people want next? But not everything people like fits Archie McPhee — you'll never find us selling pants even though everyone seems to enjoy them. It has to be something that people love, that the mere mention of makes them smile and yet seems so silly they are surprised that a company would actually spend time designing products around it. Usually it's something that they started liking before their cynical adult brain took over and dismissed. Most of the themes in this chapter come from that same goofy place.

You can count on us to keep on top of the next big thing no matter what it is. Evil Bunnies? Lepers? Canadians? The mind boggles.

### Catalog #65:
Slip this sparkly Lucha Libre Wrestling Mask over your head and instantly transform into a savage, grunting, snorting *luchador* (wrestler). It fastens with a Velcro strip in the back to make sure that your identity remains hidden while you dance around in knee-high boots and a pair of speedos.

Wrestling Mask, 2000

# LUCHA LIBRE

While the mysterious *luchadores* of Mexican wrestling are familiar to most people, few have intimate knowledge of actual wrestlers and the masked characters they portray. Our wrestlers are generic icons that represent the whole sport rather than individual participants. Still, the oddness of the products has attracted a considerable following. The bizarre and kitschy Lucha Libre Nodder has become somewhat of a cult novelty that is often spotted in the studios of prominent recording artists and designers.

Windup Head, 2000

Sproing, 2000

Nodder, 1999

# What Were We Thinking?

Remember the Sumo fad of 1999? Well neither do we, because it never happened. We sure thought it would, though. We rushed a whole line of Sumo products out to meet the probable future demand. Especially painful was the failure of our Sumo Limoges. A tiny ceramic Sumo wrestler that opened to reveal rice and chopsticks inside, it's probably my favorite of all the items we have ever produced. That this product failed caused me to doubt the taste and intelligence of my fellow humans. What hope do we have for the future when no on recognizes the awesome beauty of the Sumo Limoges?

Cookie Jar, 1999

Lunchbox, 1998

Limoges, 1998

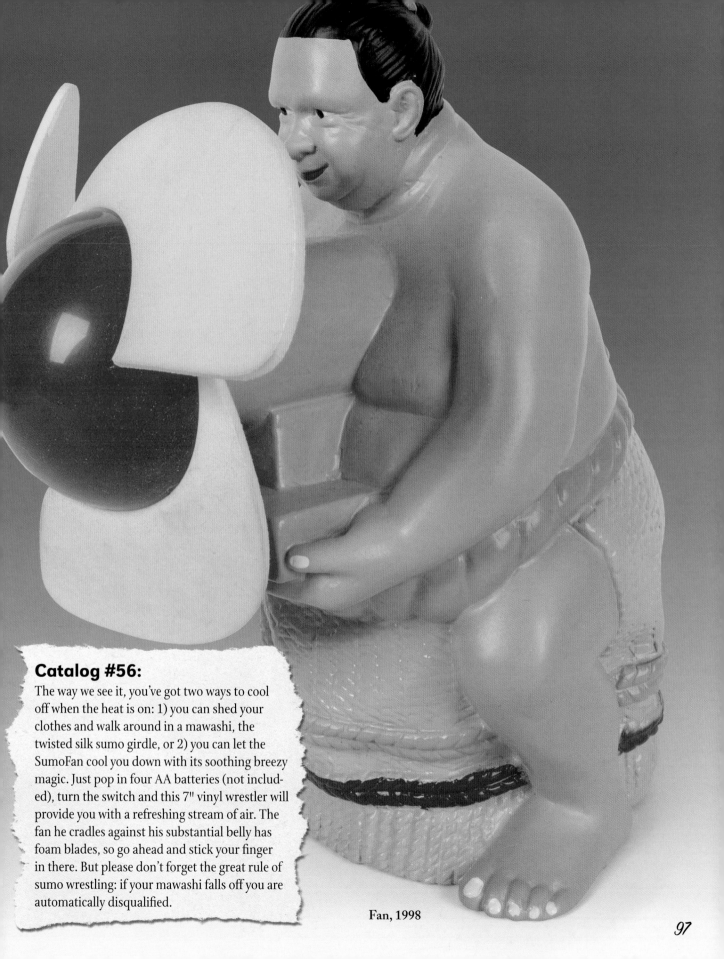

## Catalog #56:

The way we see it, you've got two ways to cool off when the heat is on: 1) you can shed your clothes and walk around in a mawashi, the twisted silk sumo girdle, or 2) you can let the SumoFan cool you down with its soothing breezy magic. Just pop in four AA batteries (not included), turn the switch and this 7" vinyl wrestler will provide you with a refreshing stream of air. The fan he cradles against his substantial belly has foam blades, so go ahead and stick your finger in there. But please don't forget the great rule of sumo wrestling: if your mawashi falls off you are automatically disqualified.

Fan, 1998

# DEVILS

Sure, devils are evil, supernatural beings who punish you for your sins, but they look so damned cool. We used a cute and cartoony style for our devil products in an attempt to make them come across as more naughty than evil. After a brief surge of popularity, the devil theme cooled off, but we expect it will come around again. Oddly enough, our devil related products are the only religious products we produce that we have never had a complaint about.

Devil Girl
Nodder, 2001

Hair Picks, 2001

Bicycle Horn, 2000

Punching Puppet, 1999

## Catalog #67:

Quit slacking! Hang the Devil Clock in your home or office as a subtle reminder that idle hands are the Devil's workshop. This 7" x 12" EVA plastic clock feels like firm foam and has hairy accents, a yellow pitchfork second hand, and a lush goatee that swings to and fro. Consider the evils of wasting time while the Devil smiles down on you with his devastatingly white grin.

Clock, 2001

# BACON

Unless you find it distasteful for moral, health or religious reasons, bacon is the most awesome food in the world. How many foods could support an entire line of novelty products? It began with the explosive popularity of the bacon bandages and hasn't slowed down since. In fact, we expect sales to remain high until our customers die of heart disease — delicious, salty heart disease.

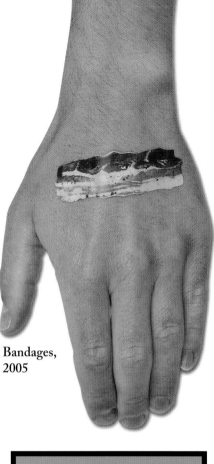

Bandages, 2005

Patron Saint of Bacon, 2007

Bacon Dental Floss, 2008

Bacon Wallet, 2006

Gummy Bacon, 2006

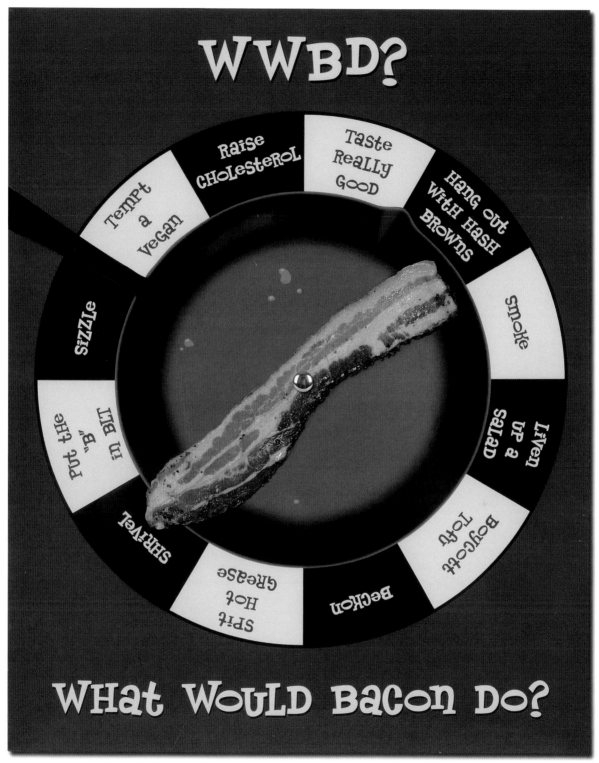

Bacon Spin Folder, 2006

**Website:**

Decisions are hard. Bacon is tasty. This 9½" x 12" glossy folder gives you a way to distract yourself from important decisions by contemplating the versatility of your favorite cured meat. Features classic spinner technology; just flick the spinner and watch it twirl round and round before stopping on an answer.

# UNICORNS

Unicorns represent all that is peaceful and serene in the world. It's only natural that they would defend us against life's minor irritations, which is why the idea of an Avenging Unicorn spearing a mime seems so natural and fulfilling. In creating more unicorn products we found that adding a unicorn to any situation instantly makes it less stressful. As you can see, we have successfully applied unicorns to the cold war and the eternal battle of good and evil. We believe that unicorns just might be the key to world peace.

Good & Evil Unicorns, 2006

Avenging Unicorn, 2005

**Catalog #73:**

The Cold War Unicorns Play Set allows you to play out the intense struggle between two global superpowers in the majestic fantasy world of the Unicorn! Can the Communist Unicorn's horn of classless social structure hold up against the Freedom Unicorn's hooves of capitalist opportunity? Each hard vinyl unicorn is 3¾" tall with articulated joints for all sorts of dramatic poses.

Cold War Unicorns, 2006

Mini Fairy Land, 2005

Unicorn Dream Oil Painting, 2005

Latex Unicorn with Glow Horn, 2007

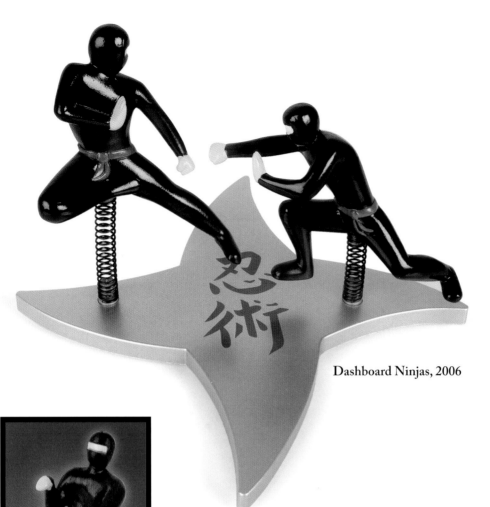

Dashboard Ninjas, 2006

# NINJAS

The more we tell you about ninjas, the more we put ourselves in danger for doing so. We tried to design our line of ninja products in such a way that no actual ninjas would take offense. So far, so good.

Bandages, 2005

Mini Ninjas, 2005

Clock, 2006

©ACCOUTREMENTS

**Catalog #73:**

It's pretty much common knowledge that ninjas control time. Just when you think you've got one in a bad spot, he'll stop time and you'll wake up three days later in the engine room of a Chinese cargo ship with double vision and a mysterious rash. This 13" tall, plastic time piece features nunchuck hands and a swinging ninja pendulum.

Tickles Figurine, 2004

# What Were We Thinking?

**Holly Hostess**

The cute Japanese characters of Sanrio® have been extremely popular for over 30 years. Based on their success, we decided to design our own cast of cute characters with a slight twist. Instead of the typical cats, dogs, birds and frogs, we created parasites.

At the time, the idea seemed brilliant. They weren't intended for children, our characters were for cynical adults and teenagers. To make them seem even more Japanese we wrote the packaging in Engrish (English that sounds as if it were badly translated from Japanese), and even created a strange back story to further explain the concept. It turned out to be a bad idea on top of a bad idea. Our customers were confused and some even sent us letters pointing out all the errors.

The strange thing was that everyone seemed to like them, but no one bought them. Adults appreciated the humor but didn't want to own them. Teenagers liked them as an irreverent alternative to Hello Kitty but didn't want to spend their money on them and kids were drawn to their cuteness but couldn't convince their parents to buy them. In the end, we were left with a warehouse full of cheap school supplies and a greater respect for the un-paralleled success and influence of the Sanrio enterprise.

## PARASITE PALS STORY

One day Holly was a lonely girl with not the friend. But she notice a feeling of itching on the head so must attend the doctor. The doctor gives the full test then believing the infection of many parasite. He give the pills for removal of the para-sites, but Holly is sad. Why to kill the parasites? Why not for them to be friends? So she was giving them each a name and now we believe she become happy. The Parasite Pals give some irritation, but much fun and love is to be shared.

Pencil Toppers, 2004

**Blinky Eyelash Mite**

**Zzeezz Bed Bug**

**Tickles Tapeworm**

**Dig Dig Head Louse**

# COCKTAIL

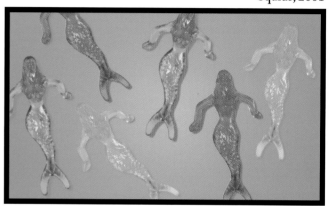

Squids, 2001

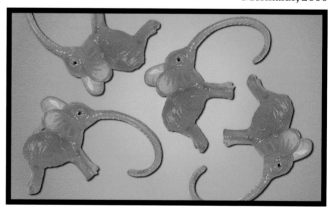

Mermaids, 2000

Demons, 2004

Pink Elephants, 2001

Black Cats, 2003

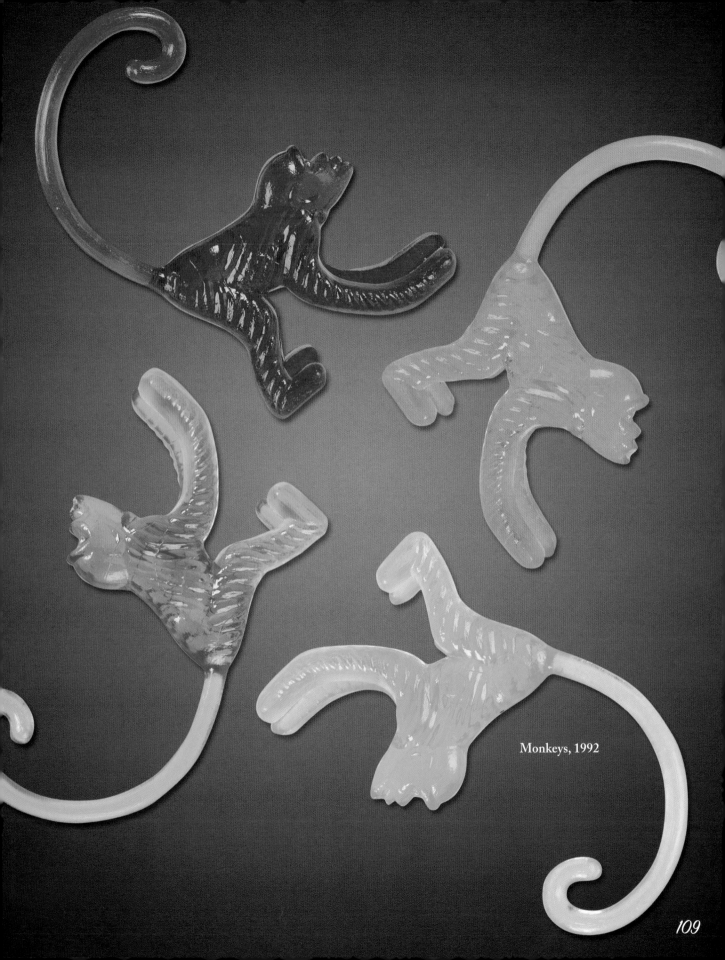

Monkeys, 1992

**Pink Elephant Shot Glasses, 2004**

## Website:

These shot glasses feature six different retro illustrations that chronicle the wild evening of a particularly party-prone pink elephant. Each set includes six 1.5 ounce glasses.

## Catalog #33:

"Why no eyes?" is what your friends and neighbors will say when they see your elegant monumental Easter Island God statue. You will never be rendered speechless because our statue comes with a wallet sized fact card that de-mystifies this most mysterious object. You'll fascinate your friends with the answers to the eye question and any others they might have. Standing solid at 6¾" tall. His coolness is made of sturdy, stone-like material.

Easter Island God, 1994

# MONKEYS

We love monkeys. And although it's politically incorrect to say so, we love monkeys in people clothes even more. The monkey with fez has been a staple in our line for years. It's one of the classic images of pop culture, but no one really knows why it's funny. It just is. We added even more humor to our monkey in fez pencil topper by giving him the old fashioned name, Karl. He's a monkey, he's in a Fez and his name is Karl. This is known as a hat-trick of hilarity. By the way, the words "monkey" and "chimpanzee" are not synonymous in the zoological world, but in the novelty world all simians fall into the monkey category.

Karl, the Pencil Monkey, 2005

Lucky Monkey, 1988

### Catalog #11:

A very lovely and large rubber monkey, crafted by hand, with emphasis on detail and quality. There are 2 different styles and each one has a golden elastic loop for hanging. The ancient Chinese believed hanging 22 of these around your front door would bring 50 gold bars and lots of good luck to the household.

Monkey with Fez
Nodder, 2000

113

Monkey with Fez
Candle, 1996

Monkey with Fez Salt & Pepper Shakers, 1998

Monkey with Fez
Swizzle Stick, 2000

Smoking Monkey, 2003

### Catalog #57:

After years observing monkeys in their natural jungle habitat, we know one thing for certain: a monkey looks silly wearing a fez. Made of high-quality, textured paraffin wax, our monkey proudly displays a bright red fez while relaxing in a comfortable squatting position. No deep symbolism, no underlying meaning, just a 7½" primate wearing a tasseled cap. Now that's funny.

Rubber Gorilla, 1990

## Catalog #17:

BIG! This gorilla is wonderful and has captured the hearts of most of the employees here. Ferocious but friendly, pliable and hollow. An entire small rodent would fit inside him without the head even sticking out. We fill him with all sorts of stuff. His body is black heavy rubber, textured with deep grooves that make him look hairy, as King Kong should. Green eyes, white teeth, huge mouth, long arms, great detail. If you are a miniature Fay Wray, watch out.

## Catalog #56:

In the wild, gorillas sharpen bamboo rods with their teeth to fish termites out of termite hills. In the office you can use that same gorilla technology to keep all your pencils nice and pointy. This 6" tall plastic pencil sharpener with soft rubber head sharpens your pencils as the terrifying jaws of the gorilla gnash and his eyes glow red with primate fury. His unholy howls (actually the sound of an electric sharpener hidden in the base) will haunt your dreams and nightmares!

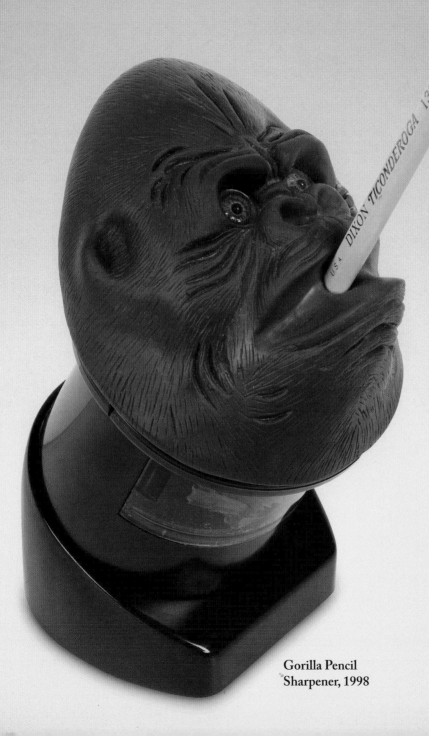

Gorilla Pencil
Sharpener, 1998

## Catalog #5:

This is a classic. Squeeze the bulb and by magic the 3" tall monkey beats away on his metal drum. If you can figure out how this works it could replace oil as an energy source and save the world from pollution. Get to work.

Drummer Monkey, 1987

Ceramic Baboon Box, 1998

## Catalog #60:

Many Westerners know them as that ugly monkey with the red bottom, but to the ancient Egyptians, baboons were the incarnation of Thoth, the god of wisdom, learning and magic. Molded in the shape of the sacred baboon's head, this 2½" treasure box can hold the tiny trinkets you hold dear. Just remember, as any Pharaoh will attest, you can't take it with you.

## Catalog #72:

Is it a cute souvenir from a third world country or a fourth grade art project? Whatever you call it, it's one of the strangest things we've ever seen. Each 7½" monkey statue is entirely covered with tiny seashells except for the paws, face and tail. Quite possibly the best white elephant gift in the history of time.

Flock Faced
Shell Monkey, 2005

118

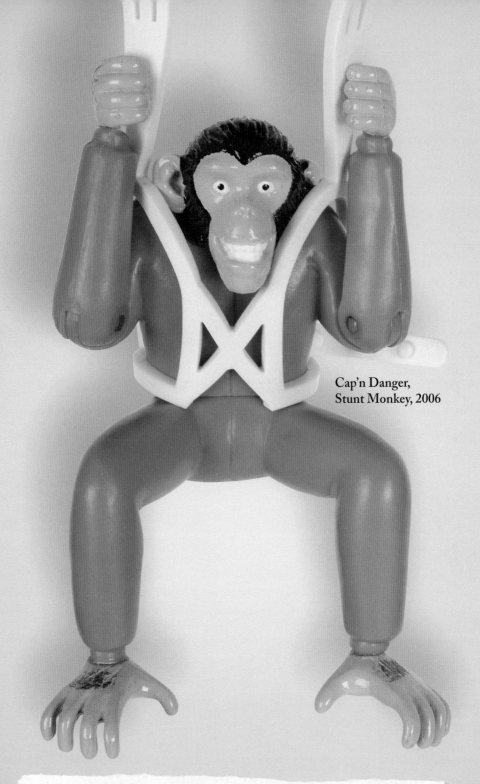

Cap'n Danger,
Stunt Monkey, 2006

## Catalog #73:

He's a parachuting primate who laughs in the face of fear; he performs outrageous stunts while grinning ear to ear! Each 4" tall, hard vinyl Cap'n Danger comes with a 26" round nylon parachute with a rubber harness. Drop him from a tall building or throw him into the air and his chute will open, allowing him to safely float to the ground. Harness fits most of our action figures!

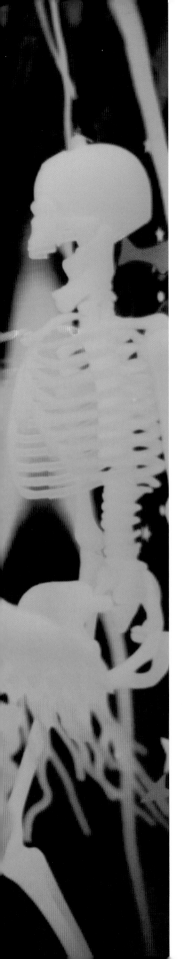

# GLOW, SQUEAK, SQUIRT, & WINDUP

In the novelty business there are a few sure-fire adjectives you can add to the name of any product to get a completely new product. For instance, you can double the size of your line of plastic fish by making another version of them that glows in the dark. If you run out of nun products that actually seem to make sense, why not make a Squeak Nun? If it's hollow and made of soft, pliable rubber, just slap the word "squirt" onto the name and you've doubled its value. And if something makes people laugh, it will make them laugh even harder if you can make it move when they wind it up.

Although we have made products that include more than one of these traits, we have yet to create something that incorporates all of them. We're not sure if the world is ready for that… yet.

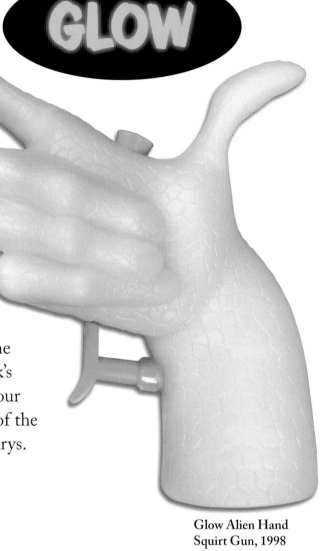

**GLOW**

We could go into detail about how the process of phosphorescence works and how studying it led to the discovery of radioactivity, but that's what Wikipedia is for. We just know that things that glow in the dark are empirically superior to things that don't. We even helped develop a high glow standard known as "turbo glow" that was featured in some of our products. The glow was so bright you could use it to read under the covers. During the height of glow-in-the-dark's popularity, when you turned out the lights in our warehouse you could still make your way out of the building by the light of a thousand Virgin Marys.

Glow Alien Hand
Squirt Gun, 1998

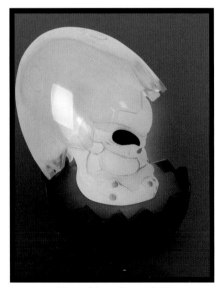

Glow Alien Egg, 1997

Glow Maria, 1996

Glow Fairies, 2006

Glow Monster Heads,
1994

## Catalog #34:

At least if you met these monsters in a dark alley
you'd see them coming because they glow in the
dark. Run before you see the whites of their eyes
because they also squirt! These frightening flesh
crawlers fire up to five feet. Use the submerge and
fill method to load up on liquid ammunition and
fire a round from each of these four different 2" tall
horned headed hobgoblins.

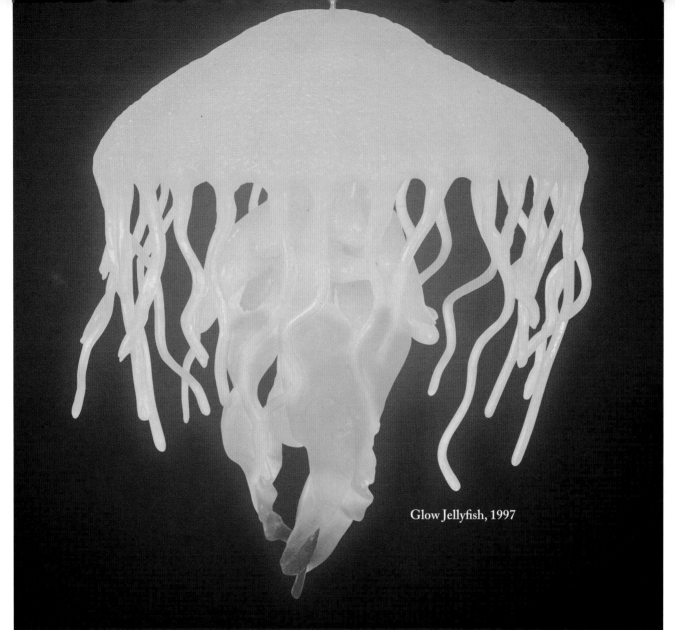

Glow Jellyfish, 1997

Glow Octopus, 1988

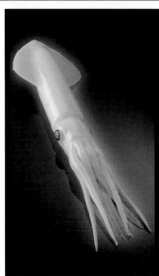

Glow Squid, 1986

Glow Pufferfish, 2006

# What Were We Thinking?

This product is proof that just because you can do something, it doesn't mean you should. Two of our best selling items were Glow String and Glowing Eyeballs. One day they were out on a table together and someone said, "Hey, together those look like spaghetti and meatballs. We should sell that!" It was really easy to design. All we had to do was make a new package and have them leave the pupil off the eye. Simple! The problem was that no one was looking for inedible, glowing spaghetti and meatballs.

WARNING: CHOKING HAZARD. PRODUCT INCLUDES SMALL BALLS. NOT FOR

Debuted, 1999

# WINDUP

Clockwork toys have been produced for centuries, but most companies never get past the basic windup animals. When we choose a windup we like to look for something bizarre and unlikely. One of our favorites was the Windup Running Nose which was not only fun to watch waddle across a table, but a cringe-worthy visual pun as well. Occasionally, as in the case of the Fish Out Of Water, the mechanism suggests the product. What else could we do with a mechanism that just flops around?

Pig Head, 1998

Robot 7, 1997

Fish Out of Water, 2000

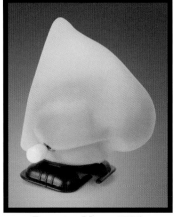

Running Nose, 1995

Spark Dino, 1985

**Catalog #39:**

Run! Hide! Evacuate the downtown area! Our 3" tall Spark Dino shoots fiery sparks from his mouth as he trudges toward the city of your choice. Star in your own home B-movies with this magnificent mobile monster. You won't even have to colorize them, because our vividly colored Spark Dino is made of bright green and yellow plastic with a fierce red mouth.

Squeak Bibo, 1994

Squeak Nun, 1996

# SQUEAK

The addition of a squeaker can make a product extremely entertaining or extremely annoying, depending on who's doing the squeaking. During our "squeak" phase, we added squeakers to everything from lobsters to pickles. We also discovered that each squeak product has its own unique sound which inspired some employees to create a Squeak Aptitude Test to see who was best at identifying a product by its squeak. Although this skill is of no value outside of Archie McPhee, the ability to identify the plaintive, mournful wail of a Squeak Rat is prized within the company. It's also a great way to impress new employees.

Squeak Pickle, 1988

Squeak Rat, 2004

**Catalog #45:**
Scuttling about in the shallows of the ocean, the squeak lobsters go about their daily routine of hunting for small crabs and worms. When the sun sets they sometimes gather to squeak campfire songs and reminisce. These lovable 8" rubber decapods are painted in glossy brown and burnt orange with pale yellow underbellies. They have spiny backs, long dangling antennae and a clear mellifluous squeak. You get two whole lobsters for the price of one lobster tail in Las Vegas.

Squeak
Lobster, 1996

# SQUIRT

From classic gags like the trick camera to all manner of sea creatures, we've had great success with squirt products. However, we took the squirt category to a whole new level with the introduction of the squirt brain. The exquisite detail and powerful stream made it a popular choice for squirting the squeamish.

Squirt Brain, 1996

Squirt Cuttlefish, 1998

Squirt Camera, 1989

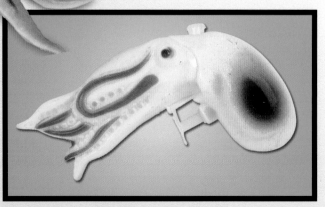

Squid Squirt Gun, 1986

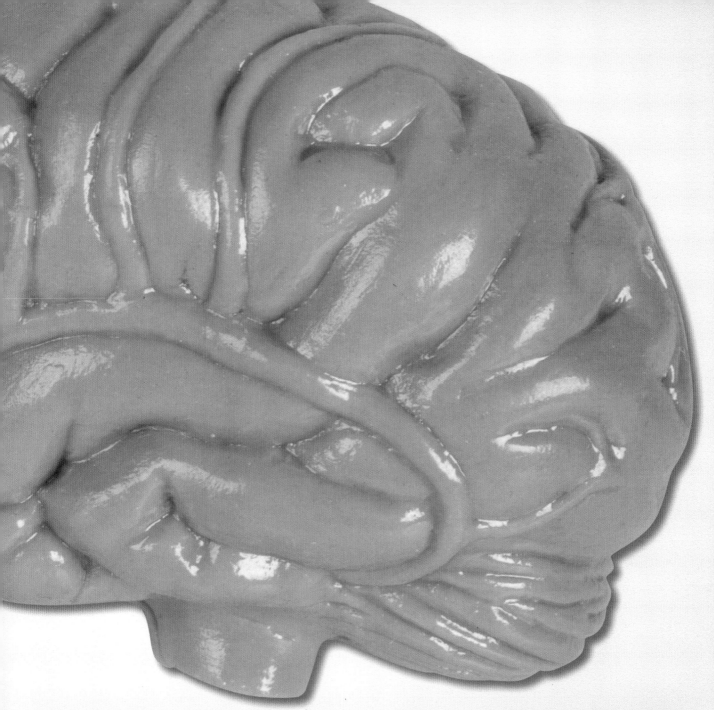

Spit Toad, 1997

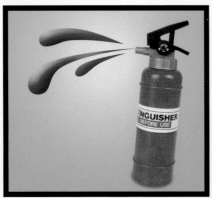

Squirt Fire Extinguisher, 1992

Squirt Ray Guns, 1994

# MCPHEE THEOLOGY

**M**ost companies avoid making novelty religious products for fear of offending people. That's fine with us, as we've been selling religious products for years to the delight of customers of all religions. As crazy as it may seem to the zealots, products that good-naturedly poke fun at religion have always done well for us.

Sure we've had complaints, but we've received far more praises. In fact, we've found that some of the most devout followers are capable of having a sense of humor about their religion. Customers have sent us stories about pastors using the Jesus Action Figure during sermons, Catholics giving out Nun Finger Puppets as party favors and Buddhists making shrines for the Squeak Monk. Our religious products give people the opportunity to have fun with their spirituality, and besides, it's a lot easier to find meaning in an action figure or finger puppet than in some of those religious texts.

"This is distasteful in the extreme. I can't see how rolling a plastic toy on the floor is going to induce religious understanding in anyone. Is it so that they can make a fool of Jesus? Stick it on your desk as a toy? Stick pins in it — that kind of pathetic behaviour? There are a lot of twisted folk going about."

– The Rev Alex Cunningham,
clerk to Glasgow Presbytery

## Catalog #67:

Everyone has a different take on Jesus. Muslims saw him as a prophet; Buddhists say he was enlightened; Hindus consider him an avatar (the incarnation of a deity in human form) while Christians hail him as the Son of God. But, wherever your theological compass points, you will agree that this is the coolest action figure since GI Joe. Each hard plastic Jesus Action Figure stands 5" tall with posable arms to reach toward the heavens and wheels in his base for smooth gliding action.

Original Action
Figure, 2001

134

# JESUS ACTION FIGURE

When the idea came up to start a line of action figures, there was one name at the top of everybody's list, Jesus. Not only is he of historical significance, he's also popular and wears a robe, which meant his legs wouldn't have to be articulated. We made the packaging as neutral as possible, covering the back with quotes from the Bible. He sold like gangbusters. So much so that we decided to upgrade him with a deluxe edition featuring glow-in-the-dark "miracle hands." Unfortunately the factory screwed up the first shipment of Deluxe Jesus and we got in a red-eyed, green-handed zombie Jesus that looked like he was hungrier for brains than he was for saving souls. Thankfully, the factory fixed the mistake and those mutant Jesuses are now just a distant, highly collectible, memory.

**Loaves and Fishes**

Deluxe Action Figure, 2005

# CATHOLICISM

The Catholic Church is the largest religious organization in the world and one of the oldest. Most of our Catholic items are caricatures of nuns that tap into nostalgic feelings people have about being raised Catholic, but other products are simple modernizations of ancient images. Take, for example, St. Clare, the patron saint of television. Originally just a realistic statue of Clare, we decided to make it glow, which seemed appropriate given her association with television. Eventually, we gave her a complete makeover in a colorful Byzantine style. We have had no official word on whether changing her image has made prayers to her more successful, but television has certainly not improved.

Nunzilla, 1997

Original Saint Clare, 1992

Glow Saint Clare, 1998

Our Exclusive Saint Clare, 2006

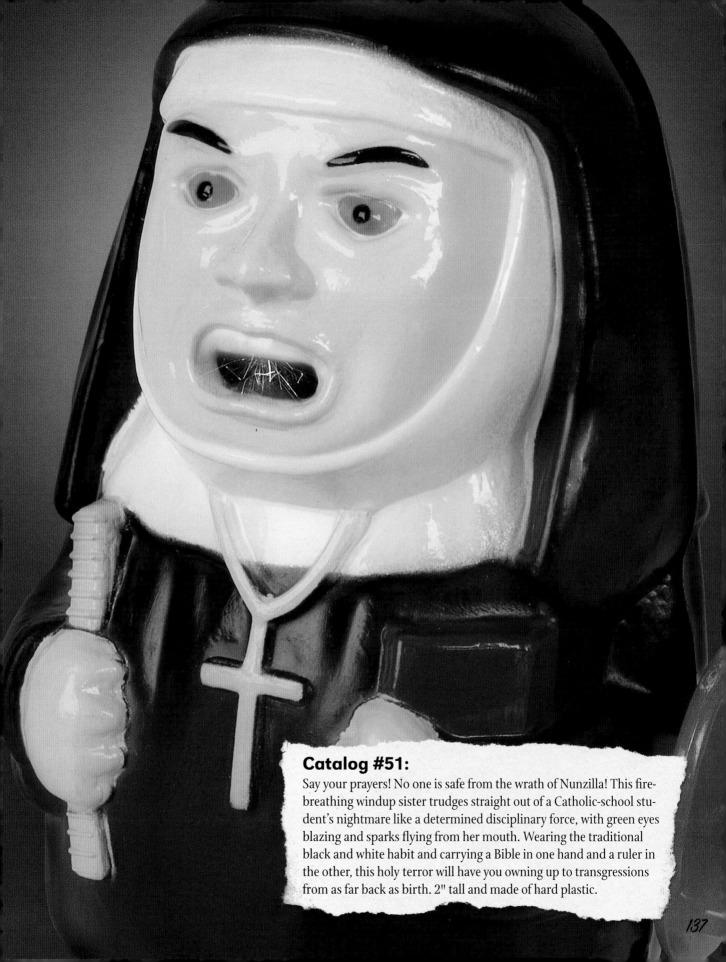

## Catalog #51:

Say your prayers! No one is safe from the wrath of Nunzilla! This fire-breathing windup sister trudges straight out of a Catholic-school student's nightmare like a determined disciplinary force, with green eyes blazing and sparks flying from her mouth. Wearing the traditional black and white habit and carrying a Bible in one hand and a ruler in the other, this holy terror will have you owning up to transgressions from as far back as birth. 2" tall and made of hard plastic.

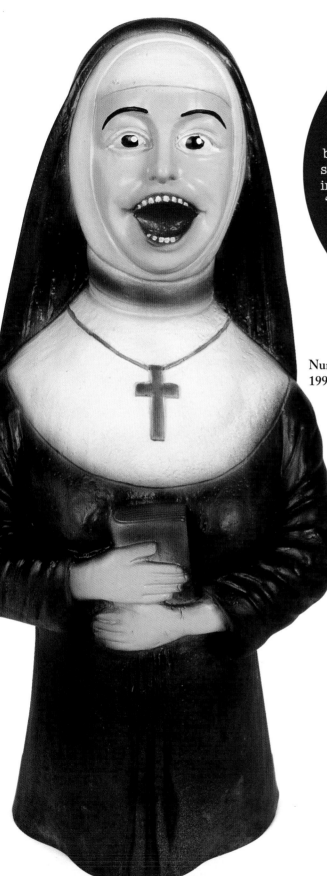

"Archie McPhee, which bills it-
self as 'Outfitters of Popular Culture,'
included in its 'Collector's Edition Catalog'
a number of items which caricatured Catholic
nuns, some quite offensively. For example, there
was a windup doll, 'Nunzilla,' billed as 'Terrifying,
but in a good way.' 'Say your prayers,' the ad in-
structs. Other items included the 'Fighting Nun Punching Puppet,' wearing boxing gloves and headlined,
'Punch you. Bless you. Punch you. Bless you'; and
'Sing it, sister,' a rubber hand puppet that 'can also
act as an insulating glove while working with
toxic chemicals or lepers.' "

– 1997 Catholic League Report
on Anti-Catholicism

Nun Hand Puppet,
1997

Catholic School Salt & Pepper Shakers, 1998

**Catalog #42:**

If this doesn't make you feel secure at night, what will? The white plastic figure of the Virgin Mary is 5¾" tall on a 1" base. Just remember to say to yourself before going to bed, "I have a new Mary Night Light, I have a new Mary Night Light," or you may wake up disoriented in the middle of the night and think you've seen the holiest vision since Lourdes. The plug-in base has an on/off switch, uses one appliance bulb (included), and swivels for added watchfulness.

Glow Mary
Night Light, 1996

139

# BUDDHISM

As I was leaving a fantastic seafood restaurant in Taiwan, I saw a Buddhist monk sitting beside the road talking on a cell phone and drinking a latte. It struck me as the perfect mix of the spiritual and material as well as the ancient and modern coexisting in a middle path of perfect harmony. We recreated the moment in plastic, added a squeaker and created a symbol of the search for peace in a world of distractions. The response from our customers was transcendent.

Happy Squeak
Monk, 1995

### Catalog #62:
Every modern Buddhist knows that Nirvana can be reached much more quickly and efficiently over the internet than by the old methods. This 3½" wide, 5" tall soft vinyl Buddha sits peacefully gazing at his laptop computer. The reverent look on his face shows that he is pleased with the spiritual convenience of modern technology. Give him a squeeze and he'll squeak!

Squeak Laptop
Buddha, 1999

Dear Satan Mcphee,

Some of your products express the most aggressive behavior to look down on the Lord Buddha. So I hope Buddhists all around the world will prayer [sic] for your company demolition. In addition, all your family will get the most severe diseases.

– Customer complaint

Dog & Cat Buddhas,
1997

141

# HINDUISM

Hinduism is a complex and ancient religion with multiple gods. Admittedly, part of what attracted us to developing Hindu products was the strangeness of it, but the main reason was the beauty and color of Hindu art. As a matter of fact, our first Hindu related products were reproductions of that stunning art on lunch boxes. Eventually we moved on to creating our own custom products. There hasn't been much complaint about these, and what we have had has been polite and well reasoned. We did make the Hindu Human Rights Group's "Gallery of Hindu Imagery Abuse," but honestly, our stuff doesn't look that bad next to Krishna underwear.

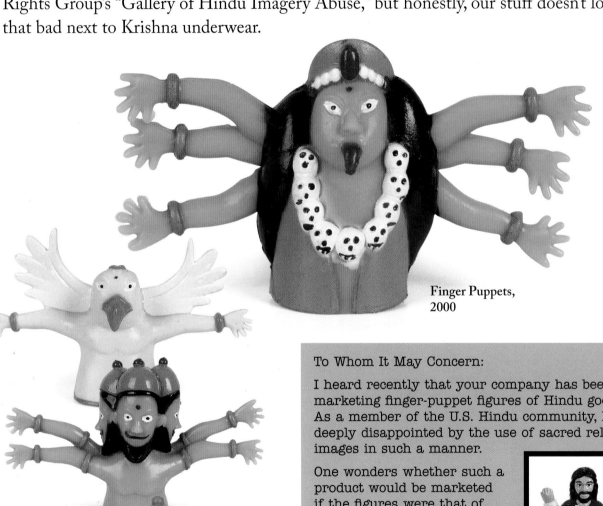

Finger Puppets,
2000

To Whom It May Concern:

I heard recently that your company has been marketing finger-puppet figures of Hindu gods. As a member of the U.S. Hindu community, I am deeply disappointed by the use of sacred religious images in such a manner.

One wonders whether such a product would be marketed if the figures were that of the Judeo-Christian tradition, such as Jesus Christ, Mary, Moses, etc.

I urge you to reconsider the insensitive marketing of such products.

– Customer complaint

Jesus Pencil Topper,
2005

**Catalog #63:**
This striking candle holder is perfect to set just the right mood for your next deep meditation or spiritual journey. A Hindu deity sits in a tranquil pose with arms outstretched, holding a standard sized candle (not included) in each hand.

Candle Holder, 1999

*143*

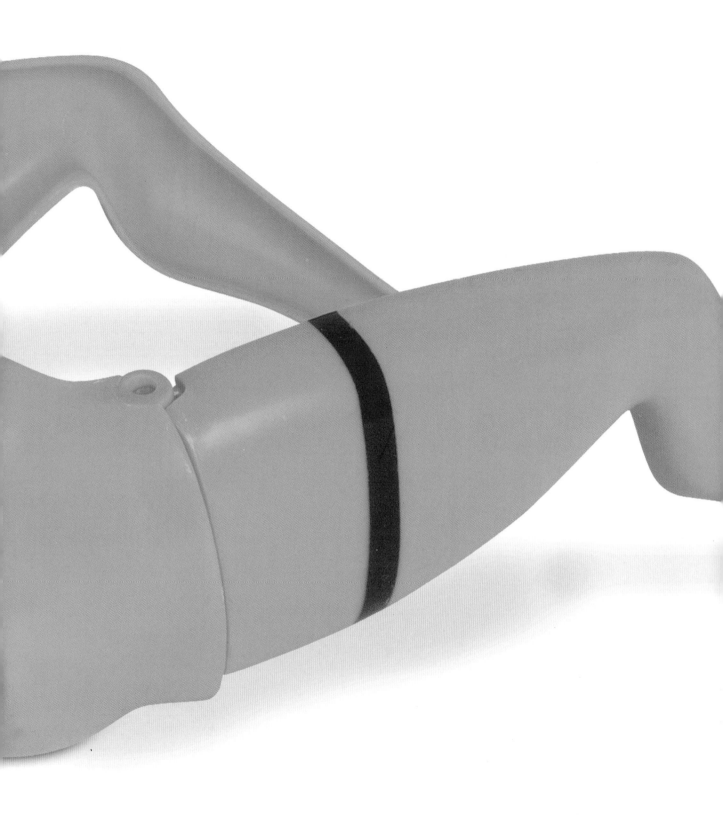

144

# GONE,
# BUT NOT FORGOTTEN

We don't miss every product that gets dropped from our line. No one is mourning the loss of our Mini Gardening Tools or Neon Chess Set. But there are products that either leave before their time because of circumstances beyond our control or that sell so badly we can't justify keeping them around no matter how much we love them.

This section is our tribute to those products that still have a special place in our hearts even though they are gone from our warehouse.

# HAND CHAIR

The hand chair had a dirty secret that will make you want to scrub it with anti-bacterial soap. The company that manufactured it primarily made septic tanks. During the molding process they were left with a lot of waste plastic that they had to pay to have taken away. Someone on their staff came up with the idea of using the excess plastic to make chairs in the shape of hands. These chairs were very popular, but we had to discontinue them when rising shipping costs made it impossible to send them out.

Debuted 1998

## Catalog #56:

These attractive 3 ft. tall hard plastic hand chairs weigh over 24 lbs. and are surprisingly comfortable. They are perfect porch furniture or lovely in the living room. At the office, you can use one to make anyone who sits in it feel as tiny and helpless as a newborn babe. No one can negotiate professionally while their rump is being cupped by a giant hand. If you find a glove large enough, you can even get your chair upholstered. Comes in fake granite style.

# BOBBY LUCEY

Designed by my daughter Lily Pahlow, when she was very young, Bobby Lucey was her imaginary friend made real. This is the best designed product ever produced and should have won all kinds of awards.

**Catalog #58:**

It's animal, mineral, and vegetable. It's a bendy, a doll, and an action figure. The elusive Bobby Lucey is nothing in particular or anything you want. The whole story behind Bobby Lucey is slowly being unlocked from the cryptic records found in a pile of clippings on the barber shop floor. This omnifarious 7" wonder (wonder what it is), comes in a variety of colors.

Debuted 1998

# HEAD SHARPENERS

## Catalog #20:

Bizarre caricatures! 2" tall. Hand painted and flesh-colored. (Mark says if we want to make sure what these are made of that we could smash one with a hammer. But that then we'd have to pay for it. We think he was kidding!) Interesting and slightly startling desk accessories. We love them!

**Debuted 1991**

# SIN GLASSES

Debuted 1985

# ROLI ZOLI

Debuted 1986

# FRILLED LIZARD

The Australian Frilled Lizard with its fierce, pleated ruff extended around its neck was our most popular nature product of all time. In fact, it became one of the symbols of our company. We used it in one of our logos, put it on our stationery and even had a large bust of it made to hang on the front of our retail store in Seattle.

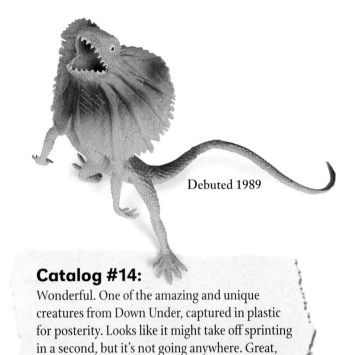

Debuted 1989

## Catalog #14:

Wonderful. One of the amazing and unique creatures from Down Under, captured in plastic for posterity. Looks like it might take off sprinting in a second, but it's not going anywhere. Great, careful detail. 8" tall.

# LOCH NESS SALT & PEPPER SHAKERS

Debuted 1998

## Catalog #58:

The Loch Ness monster: modern-day dinosaur or too much Scottish whisky on a moonlit night? Now you can ponder this question while seasoning your steak at the dinner table. Introducing the Loch Ness salt, pepper and "mystery spice" shaker set. What will that third spice be? Crushed basil, tarragon, chili pepper — the possibilities are endless. These 2½"–3" green ceramic shakers are plugged with plastic stoppers in their bottoms and have two holes on top for a controlled spice flow.

# JUVENILE DELINQUENT LOCK BOX

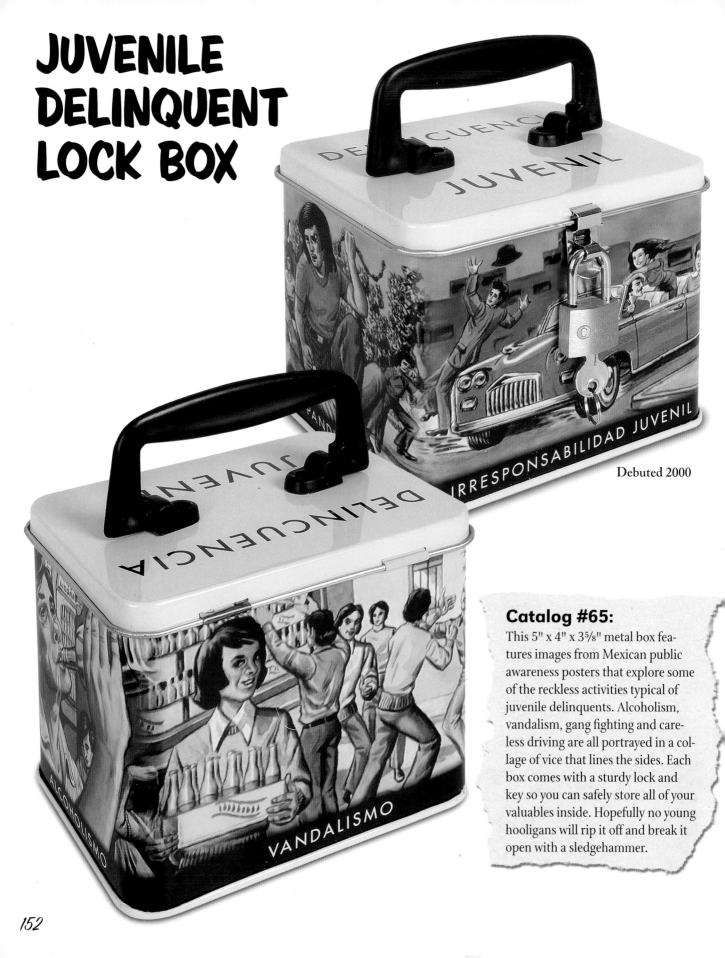

Debuted 2000

## Catalog #65:

This 5" x 4" x 3⅝" metal box features images from Mexican public awareness posters that explore some of the reckless activities typical of juvenile delinquents. Alcoholism, vandalism, gang fighting and careless driving are all portrayed in a collage of vice that lines the sides. Each box comes with a sturdy lock and key so you can safely store all of your valuables inside. Hopefully no young hooligans will rip it off and break it open with a sledgehammer.

# What Were We Thinking?

There is a long tradition of novelties that make fun of just about every embarrassing part and function of the body. From mucus to flatulence, nothing has escaped the eye of the practical joker. Well, except one thing. No one had ever made fake nose hair. We initially thought we might just sell plugs that you stuck up your nose, but that seemed unsanitary. So, we went with a more traditional plastic nose with braids of long black hair sticking out of the bottom of both nostrils. The first samples we got back from China didn't have black hair. The factory thought that perhaps we would prefer red, white and blue patriotic hair. You know, so we could show that we love our country. It was tempting, but we ended up sticking with the black.

We called it My Pretty Nosehair and packaged it as a children's toy. The lettering on the package and the text were all designed to evoke nostalgia for the toys of the 80s. More people looked at this product than bought it, but it was worth it to be able to say we were first.

**ORIGINAL PACKAGE**

Debuted 2000

**Catalog #6:**

A fuzzy windup dog. 4" tall and 5" long, handmade in Japan in the 1950s. Each in individual printed box. Limited stock!

Debuted 1987

# JUMPING DOG

The Jumping Dog didn't look much like an actual dog. It also looked nothing like the picture on the outside of the package. It was supposed to flip completely over, but in reality it just sadly fell forward as if drunk.

Debuted 2003

# STEREOTYPES OF THE WORLD DOLLS

These figures were sent to us as a sample and we sold them exactly as we got them. The only thing we did was name them in a way that pointed out that we were aware of how offensive they were. We can only surmise that the original purpose of the product was world peace through subtle racism.

**Catalog #70:**

It's United Nations Day at an all white school! Each 1¾", hand painted plastic figure is dressed in a stereotypical costume from a different country, but all of them have pinkish skin tones and huge round eyes. Just think of all the compliments/complaints you'll get when you display all 10 of these mildly offensive, but cute, cultural stereotypes!

# WEIRD, WEIRDER, WEIRDEST

**W**eird is in the eye of the beholder and over the years we have built up quite a resistance to weird. What might seem strange to others is just a day's work for us. The products in this chapter are so strange, bizarre and just plain odd that they even left us confused and bewildered.

Even weirder is the fact that we designed a lot of the very products that freak us out. It's one thing to discover something and question where it came from and why people would want to buy it, but it's another thing altogether to design a product that leaves you with the same questions.

Our weirdest products are the lifeblood of our company. They are exciting and inspirational beacons that power our creativity and drive us to keep pushing the boundaries of the surreal and absurd.

Also, while some of these didn't sell very well, they did attract attention to us and increase the sales of the slightly less weird products. Bibo, as you will soon discover, sets the bar for weird so high, it makes everything else we sell appear almost normal.

When I spotted the Bibo Clock in a factory showroom in Taiwan it was love at first sight. When I showed it to the rest of the employees, they loved it too. None of us understood it, but we all loved it. Overcome with curiosity, we eventually asked the factory to fax us information about this strange little guy. "The Story of Bibo" that we received only deepened our love. After finding out that Bibo was a popular figure, we knew there must be other Bibo products. We imported a squeak version of Bibo and then created our own Windup Sparking Bibo that shot sparks from his mouth. Our customers couldn't get enough of him and his fame culminated with a guest appearance on the television show *Frasier*.

BIBO! BIBO! BIBO!

## Catalog #31:

Let's see if we can explain: 1) He's a good monster. 2) His eyes jiggle when you shake him. 3) His ears are so big his head spans almost 6". 4) He cries "BEEPAH BEEPAH" (which has been interpreted as "Pizza, Pizza" by some, "Beepbop" by others). 5) When he cries a red light flashes between his eyes. 6) To get it to stop (and believe us, you'll want to) you press the cupie point on the top of his head. 7) The numbers on his clock glow-in-the-dark. Really, there is no feature on this clock that doesn't startle us.

### EXCERPT FROM "THE STORY OF BIBO"

Good day! Story of Bi-bo: Bi-bo is a god monster with intelligence. He has two big eyes, and he knows very well what people want to do. He cannot speak, but only "Bi-bo." When there is any danger happened, he will speak. The top of his head will light up and his hip will makes many colourful smoke to help him survive because this smoke is stinking and it can hinder the sight of his enemies. We love this Bi-bo very much because he always survive by using some funny ways.

Debuted 1993

# CAROUSEL SOLDIER

Debuted 2003

The relic of some unknown Chinese communist celebration, this Carousel Soldier is incredibly disconcerting for several reasons. The militarization of children is always strange to Americans, but we found it equally strange that anyone would mix a military celebration with such bright colors and ornate, flowery decoration. Don't be fooled by the heart-shaped speaker, if you look into the eyes of this child-soldier, you'll see nothing but a fixed look of adorable hatred aimed directly at us.

# BOY AND GIRL MANNEQUINS

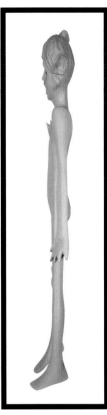

**SUPER SKINNY SIDE VIEW**

Debuted 2004

## Website:

If you took a normal, child-sized mannequin and ran it through a laundry wringer and a cartoonifier, you might get something close to these hard vinyl Boy & Girl Mannequins. Overly happy face, rigid starfish fingers and strangely flat bodies all combine to create these very weird, somewhat creepy, yet strangely appealing mannequins. The pigtailed girl stands 4' 4" tall. The blue-eyed boy is 4' 1" tall. Comes unassembled, boxed and bubble wrapped. Easy to snap together. Stand included.

# GOURD HAT

**Debuted 1995**

Made in a small town in Ohio by my brother, Scott Pahlow, these hats are examples of folk art as strange and beautiful as any Howard Finster painting. Like a prop left over from some pagan ritual to make the crops grow, the Gourd Hat is only guaranteed to do one thing: Make you look as stupid as possible.

# REMOTE CONTROL HOPPING, YODELLING LEDERHOSEN

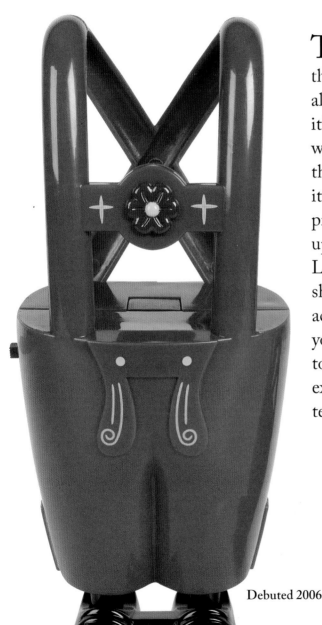

Debuted 2006

The Windup Hopping Lederhosen was an idea that kept coming up in our creative meetings. It always got a laugh, but would people actually buy it? Finally, an adamant designer drew it up and we sent the specs to the factory just to see what the prototype would look like. To our surprise, it has consistently been one of our best selling products. So much so, that we designed a follow-up, the Remote Control Hopping, Yodelling Lederhosen. It features a remote control in the shape of a knockwurst with a single button that activates the hopping and yodelling. To get the yodel, we held a yodelling contest for our customers with a prize of 100 Rubber Chickens. We expect a Nobel Prize for advancing lederhosen technology into the 21st century.

## Catalog #74:

It's the next generation of novelty lederhosen! Each 6¼" tall, plastic pair of Bavarian trousers is activated by infrared remote control technology. Just press the button on the 4½" long, plastic knockwurst and watch in joyous astonishment as the lederhosen hops around and sings a merry little yodel. Undoubtedly, one of the most absurdly hysterical products ever created.

165

# MR. BACON vs.

**Catalog #75:**
Mr. Bacon and Monsieur Tofu are fired up and ready to rumble, but only one can remain at the top of the food chain! Mr. Bacon stands 5⅝" tall and fights for everything salty, greasy and meaty. Monsieur Tofu is 3⅜" tall and represents all things made of coagulated soy milk. The winner gets eaten for dinner! Each vinyl figure has bendable arms and legs.

# MONSIEUR TOFU

Our obsession with bacon reached new heights with the Mr. Bacon vs. Monsieur Tofu Play Set. We intended to take a neutral stance with this epic rivalry, but we couldn't resist personifying tofu as a snooty Frenchman. Despite our obvious bias, the product was popular with both carnivores and vegans.

Debuted 2008

# KALI WITH NODDING TONGUE

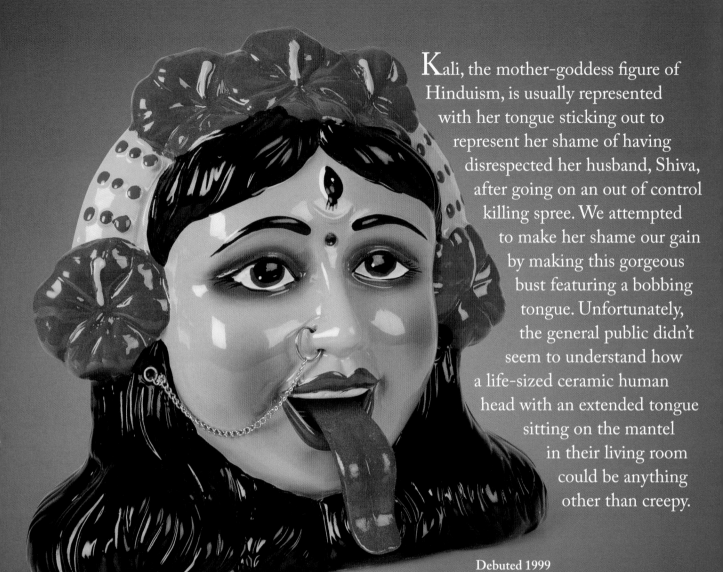

Kali, the mother-goddess figure of Hinduism, is usually represented with her tongue sticking out to represent her shame of having disrespected her husband, Shiva, after going on an out of control killing spree. We attempted to make her shame our gain by making this gorgeous bust featuring a bobbing tongue. Unfortunately, the general public didn't seem to understand how a life-sized ceramic human head with an extended tongue sitting on the mantel in their living room could be anything other than creepy.

**Debuted 1999**

## Catalog #63:

Wearing a tiara of beautiful flowers, a third eye on her forehead, and a golden hoop through her nose, Kali appears to be a lovely Indian woman. But wait: she is the goddess of destruction and renovation, with a tongue that nods on a spring! This gorgeous 8" x 8" x 5½" ceramic head is a decorative piece that is sure to get noticed with her long red tongue bobbing out of a sly smile. Kali may be beautiful, but to the believers of Hinduism she can be deadly.

# MINI GUILLOTINE

## Catalog #58:

Have your GI Joes been naughty? Punish them with the McPhee Mini Guillotine. Each 5½" guillotine is made from die-cast metal, comes on its own sturdy, stained-wood base and has a dull blade for safety reasons. A golden basket is thoughtfully placed in front to catch appendages. Severed head fact: Occasionally a displaced head will retain brain and motor functions for approximately one minute after being severed!

Debuted 1998

# MUTANT CHICKEN PUPPET

## Catalog #53:

Hands down, this is the strangest puppet we sell. 15" long from head to toe, this soft rubber hand puppet vaguely resembles a rubber chicken in that it is bright yellow-orange in color and chickenesque in form. But this chicken looks like a genetic experiment gone awry, with its bulbous, lumpy head and gaping beak, tiny flightless wings, and disproportional, dangling chicken legs. Its mouth is movable, and the flexible rubber allows you to exaggerate its deformities even more. This is the stuff nightmares are made of.

Debuted 1997

# PEE GUY

Debuted 2003

# INTERNAL ORGAN FANS

**Catalog #61:**

Regulate your body temperature with anatomical fans! These 5" tall, 4" wide fans are shaped like a human heart and pair of lungs, detailed with all the arteries and tissue that make internal organs so attractive. Attached to the front of each hollow plastic organ is a 4½" wide fan with soft foam blades. Rotate the switch on the bottom for a loving breeze from the heart or a cool exhale from the lungs. The Love Fan is an odd and slightly disturbing gift for your sweetheart while the Lung Fan makes a thoughtful and encouraging gift for smokers giving up the habit.

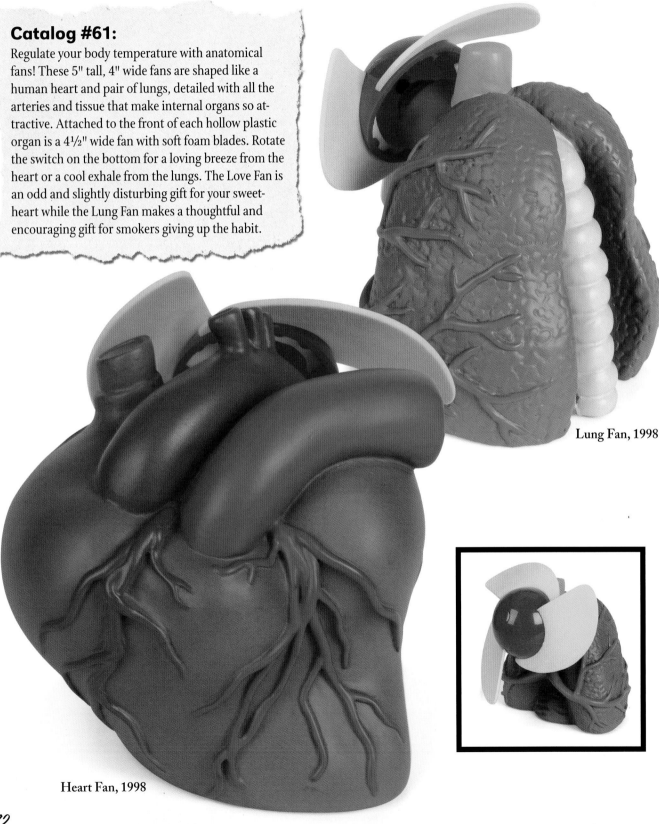

Lung Fan, 1998

Heart Fan, 1998

# LOAFMAN

## Catalog #39:

Undoubtedly the most foul item we carry! Loafman has a skeleton body, realistic skull head and (his most attractive feature) a removable loaf of SQUEAKING viscera, hence the name Loafman. This is a shining example of the human need to poke fun at what we find most frightening. It is also a good item to use to scare the pants off someone! We defy anyone, anywhere to find a petroleum-based product with squeaking entrails to equal Loafman.

**SQUEAKING VISCERA**

This skeleton with removable, squeaking loaf of guts has long been a staff favorite and for a time our customer service department would conclude each phone order with, "And would you like a Loafman with that?" When the sales of Loafman dried up, we had moderate success selling the loaf on its own under the name, "Squeak Viscera."

Debuted 1995

173

# AVENGING NARWHAL

The success of our Avenging Unicorn (page 102) got us to thinking about doing a spinoff product featuring the only naturally occurring one-horned animal, the narwhal. Since it was an actual creature, not a fantasy, we couldn't give it the same motivation for impaling as the unicorn. When we couldn't come up with anything plausible we resorted to a common technique we'd used in the past — we just made stuff up. So, in the warped world of Archie McPhee, narwhals go around impaling all creatures that are cuter than they are. Amazingly, we discovered that people didn't even know what a narwhal was and we had to start by explaining it. Never a good sign for a product that is supposed to make you laugh. The strangest responses we've had, though, are complaints saying that the story of our narwhal contributes to school shootings because it makes light of an angry loner taking revenge against better looking people. Teenagers identifying with narwhals? That had not occurred to us.

Debuted 2006

## Catalog #74:

The narwhal is an arctic-dwelling whale that has been called "the unicorn of the sea" due to its long pointy tusk. There is debate about the true purpose of this tusk, but finally the truth is revealed! The narwhal uses its tusk to impale the cute animals of the world, specifically baby seals, baby penguins and koalas. This 5½" long, hard vinyl narwhal comes with four magic tusks (crystal, onyx, ruby and ice) to impale the three 1½" long, soft vinyl cuties. Don't let cute overrun the world, fight back with your own Avenging Narwhal!

**KOALA**

**BABY SEAL**

# HELL MONEY ACCESSORY KITS

When I first arrived in China, I was intrigued by the expressions of ancestor worship (actually veneration) in everyday life. These included visiting gravesites, making offerings and keeping ancestors supplied with necessities in the afterlife.

In Chinese mythology, the dead first go to Diyu, "the underground court," which is poorly translated into English as Hell. Moreover, practical even into the afterlife, the Chinese feel their ancestors will need money and supplies.

Money is the most common item sent to ancestors. A variety of Hell Banknotes, which we have sold at the Archie McPhee store, are ceremonially burned to transfer the cash into the underworld, where it can be used to bribe officials, if required. There are also a variety of common objects made from paper and paper-mâché such as shirts, shoes, dresses, TVs, telephones, cars (Mercedes is popular), toiletries and even credit cards, that are burned and transmuted into the afterlife.

I found and imported thousands of charming boxed paper sets of personal effects. One set for a lady, containing necklaces, rings, bracelets and a Rolex® watch. Another set for a gentleman, containing a fountain pen, cuff links, rings, glasses and an Omega® watch — *all made of paper.*

When they arrived at US Customs, they were promptly seized. The little crude paper watches in each set were printed with tiny corporate logos. Charges of importation of counterfeit watches were prepared, despite the obvious.

To avoid criminal prosecution, we agreed to destroy, at our expense and at an official government incinerator, all the merchandise. Thus, on one clear, sunny Seattle day, thousands of assorted paper accessories, including Rolex® and Omega® watches, were incinerated, which was their ultimate purpose.

The financial loss of the shipment was mitigated by the delicious image of thousands of items raining from the sky in Hell and into the appreciative hands of puzzled ancestors, courtesy of the U. S. Government.

BUSTED!

Never Debuted

# TOAD PURSE

## Catalog #71:

Take this terrific toad tote with you on your next date with Prince Charming. Each 9" long purse has a soft fabric exterior and bamboo handles. Zippered pouch inside gives you plenty of room to store your stuff.

Debuted 2004

Debuted 2007

**Catalog #74:**
Unbelievably cool and completely indescribable! The fact that it exists is a tribute to the creative genius of mankind. Pipe cleaner arms, dangly plastic spring legs and a gold loop for hanging. 3½" tall.

# MIGHTY MONKEY

When I asked the factory for a sample of Mighty Monkey they were surprised and slightly embarrassed. After all, it looks like someone was sweeping the floor under the production line and used the contents of their dustpan to make a monkey. It wasn't a good product in any traditional sense and they had probably only included it to make their line look bigger. Even after we ordered it the factory kept trying to change it and make it "better" than the sample which delayed its arrival by months. But it was worth the effort, just look at him.

# YODELLING PICKLE

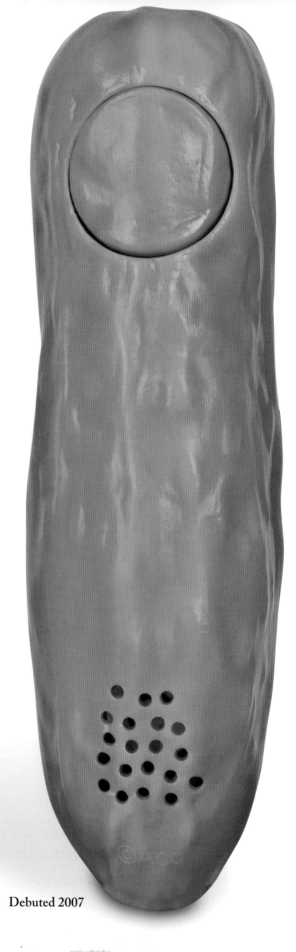

The Yodelling Pickle was born of necessity. We had to have a sound chip made for the Remote Control Hopping, Yodelling Lederhosen (page 165) and the smallest amount they would allow us to make was 30,000. This left us with a surplus of chips that we needed to figure out some way to use before they disintegrated in a warehouse. After much deliberation, we found our answer in the company refrigerator. To our delight, the Yodelling Pickle was attacked in the press for being the most wasteful and pointless product of Christmas 2007. As a result, it was our best selling product of the year, inspiring us to create even more pointless and wasteful products.

**Catalog #74:**

Are you sick and tired of trying to convince a jar of pickles to yodel using melodious mind bullets and sheer force of will? So were we. At last, the Electronic Yodelling Pickle that you have always hoped for! Each 6½" long plastic pickle yodels its little heart out at the push of a button. Batteries included.

Debuted 2007

# SURPRISE BAG

If the life of a product were a trip on a train, the Surprise Bag would be the final stop at the end of the line. As the engineer calls out for them to exit for the final time, we wrap them, our failed dreams, in brown paper and sell them to our customers at a loss. I have to admit that this is a tragedy to me. But, in the end, it must be done to clear the way for new products that will cling to the train like an army of tenacious hobos, bound for glory, hoping to escape the fate of their lost brothers.

*The object of life is not to be on the side of the majority, but to escape finding oneself in the ranks of the insane.*

—Marcus Aurelius

Debuted 1994

# ACKNOWLEDGMENTS

Special thanks and appreciation to:
Sue Aho, Kristyn Ansell, Aaron Bagley, Jessixa Bagley, S.R. & Marilyn Benton, Chris Bishop, Dinese Bjorn, Jack Broom, Rebecca Corwin, Matthew Cory, Jerilyn Davidson, Hans Dekkars, Benjamin Delgado, Jason Erickson, Marla Erwin, Scott Evans, Ken Feldman, Heather Fenech, Christian Fulghum, Robert Fulghum, Craig Garrett, Peter Gibson, Stephanie Gierman, Jean Godden, Seth Godin, Melody Goetz, Sofia Goff, Jeffrey Graham, David & Candy Gray, Louis Greenberg, Tony Greene, Andrea Greenwold, Curt Hanks, Brenda Haugaard, Gibson Holub, Diane Howell, Vivian Hsieh, Richard Hwang, Shana Iverson, Bob Jacobsen Sr., Maika Keuben, Scott King, Daisy Koo, Liandra Ferol Krebs, Molly Kuehn, Betty Larson, Nate Leson, Tao & Joan Liang, Lee Lott, Scott Luttinen, Francis & Ophelia Mak, Denise McCarrel, Anne & Mike McGilvray, Alastair McLachlan, Beth McPhee, Jan Medaska, Irving Mendoza, Deirdre Middleton, Jim Motroni, Mel Nadel, Dick Newkirk, Sandra O'Brien, Scott Pahlow, Lily Pahlow, Julia Pahlow, Jennifer Parkinson, Galan Parsons, Nancy Pearl, Jerry Pressner, Steve Quenell, Kimberly Redding, Stan Reeve, David Reinhardt, Betsy Reiss, Troy Rimstad, Kerry Rye, Cooper Rye, Kaochoy Saechao, Naigwin Saechao, Naiseng Saechao, Henk & Betse Schaap, Cori Schoenholz, Bill Shire, Perry Shore, Dena Simpson, Randy Smith, Steven Smith, Karin Snelson, Michele Stumpf, Jacqueline Sugita, Mary Sugita, Ashleigh Talbot, Chantsoy Teurn, Glenna Tollett, Mitchell Vandegrift, Jessie VanVorhis, David Wahl, Elizabeth Wallis, Kipling West, Elizabeth Whales, Kobi Yamada.

Happy Face Skeleton, 1996